Aspects of modern sociology

# The social structure of modern Britain

GENERAL EDITORS

John Barron Mays
Eleanor Rathbone Professor of Social Science, University of Liverpool

Maurice Craft
Senior Lecturer in Education, University of Exeter

BY THE SAME AUTHOR

National Insurance and Assistance in Great Britain (*1950*)
An Introduction to the Study of Social Administration (editor) (*1965*)
The Social Sciences: An Outline for the Intending Student (*1965*)
The Future of the Welfare State (*1964*)
The Changing Social Structure of England and Wales, 1871–1961
(*revised edition 1965*)

# The Welfare State

---

**D. C. Marsh,** M. Com.

Professor and Head of Department of Applied Social Science
University of Nottingham

Longman

LONGMAN GROUP LIMITED
LONDON

*Associated companies, branches and representatives throughout the world*

© *Longman Group Limited* 1970

All rights reserved. No part of this publication may be reproduced, stored in a retrieval system, or transmitted in any form or by any means, electronic, mechanical, photocopying, recording, or otherwise, without the prior permission of the Copyright owner.

*First published 1970*

ISBN 0 582 48769.2 (cased)
         48770.6 (paper)

*Printed in Great Britain by*
*Spottiswoode, Ballantyne and Co. Ltd.*
*London and Colchester*

# Contents

| | |
|---|---|
| Editors' Preface | vii |
| Acknowledgements | viii |
| 1 The evolution of the concept of a welfare state | 1 |
| 2 The creation and implementation of social policies | 22 |
| 3 Fulfilling the basic aims of a welfare state | 39 |
| 4 The decision-making and administrative problems of maintaining a welfare state | 59 |
| 5 Looking to the future | 87 |
| References and further reading | 107 |
| Index | 115 |

# Editors' Preface

British higher education is now witnessing a very rapid expansion of teaching and research in the social sciences, and, in particular, in sociology. This new series has been designed for courses offered by universities, colleges of education, colleges of technology, and colleges of further education to meet the needs of students training for social work, teaching and a wide variety of other professions. It does not attempt a comprehensive treatment of the whole field of sociology, but concentrates on the social structure of modern Britain which forms a central feature of most university and college sociology courses in this country. Its purpose is to offer an analysis of our contemporary society through the study of basic demographic, ideological and structural features, and through the study of such major social institutions as the family, education, the economic and political structure, and so on.

The aim has been to produce a series of introductory texts which will in combination form the basis for a sustained course of study, but each volume has been designed as a single whole and can be read in its own right.

We hope that the topics covered in the series will prove attractive to a wide reading public and that, in addition to students, others who wish to know more than is readily available about the nature and structure of their own society will find them of interest.

JOHN BARRON MAYS
MAURICE CRAFT

# Acknowledgements

I am grateful to Penguin Books Ltd for permission to reproduce much of the material I used in *The Future of the Welfare State*, published as a Penguin Special in 1964 and now out of print. I wish, also, to thank most sincerely Mrs M. King who in her very limited spare time typed, so expertly and expeditiously, the original manuscript of this book. All errors and imperfections are of course my responsibility.

D. C. MARSH

*Nottingham, 1969*

# The evolution of the concept of a welfare state

It is not at all certain when the phrase 'the welfare state' or even 'a welfare state' first came to be used, but by the 1950s it was commonly believed that in Britain we had, at last, arrived at a position where we were entitled to talk about our welfare state. Some other countries, notably New Zealand, Sweden and Norway had of course attained this status long before and early in the twentieth century James Bryce in his classic study of *Modern Democracies* had described New Zealand as 'the social laboratory of the world' by which he might well have meant a welfare state. But in Britain, and one suspects, elsewhere, it was uncommon to talk about 'a' or even 'the' welfare state until after the Second World War.

Yet, even now, in the 1970s, there seems to be no real consensus of opinion as to what is a welfare state and what are the principles and practices of a state which entitles it to be given this label. Certainly in Britain it would seem that most people believe we have a welfare state because we have a wide range of social services, yet if one asked the man-in-the-street to define what he means by the social services he would probably find great difficulty in giving an adequate definition. Equally, no politician in this country has yet provided an adequate description despite the fact that all political parties seem to be committed to maintaining the Welfare State.

One suspects that for most citizens and for most politicians a welfare state is one in which attempts are made to ensure reasonably high material standards of living for all. A vague description which most of us would understand in terms of our own cultural background, but surely the answer cannot be quite as simple as this? Does not the nature of the state matter, and is welfare restricted to material well-being? Could a totalitarian state which ensured the material living condition of the masses and denied them the right to freedom of thought qualify as a welfare state? Surely not, so there must be more to it than a mere concern for physical well-being.

Limiting 'welfare' to the attainment of reasonable physical standards of living is understandable in Britain where the state has most clearly revealed its changing nature and functions through its attempts to deal with the problems of financial poverty. Obviously, in a modern complex industrialised society based on division of labour an individual's standard of living depends on his ability to buy goods and services, which in turn depends, usually, on his income. In the past a major preoccupation of social reformers was to find ways of helping the poor, that is those with incomes insufficient even to maintain physical health, and the varied attempts to relieve poverty have usually been looked upon as 'welfare' measures. Relief of the poor and welfare became therefore synonymous, so that when the state extended its functions, especially in the twentieth century, so as to provide services for the relief of a variety of forms of poverty these were deemed to be welfare functions.

Attempts by the state to relieve poverty have been made for over three centuries through the Poor Laws, but it is doubtful if anyone would attach the label of 'welfare state' to the England of Queen Elizabeth I or even Victorian England. The standard of life which could be attained on the assistance granted by the Poor Law authorities was low, and perhaps even more disturbing was the fact that the standard attainable by a not inconsiderable proportion of the working population was not very much higher, even in the late nineteenth century. The revealing social surveys of Booth and Rowntree in the 1890s showed that poverty was widespread despite the unprecedented increase in material wealth which had made Britain the richest country in the world at the end of the nineteenth century. Poverty was not confined to the work-shy, the feckless, the criminal, or other undesirable elements in society. There was real poverty to be found among hard-working men and women whose wages after working long hours under intolerable conditions were insufficient to provide for a reasonable standard of life, and of course it was quite impossible for them to save in order to protect themselves in sickness, unemployment, old age, or widowhood.

The ways in which the functions of the state in Britain had been extended so as to ensure minimum levels of income in some employments and income security during periods of interruption or cessation of earnings are by now well established. Beginning with the Old Age Pensions Act 1908, the Trade Boards Act 1909, and the National Insurance Act 1911, a vast and complicated system had been evolved. The main concern of most of the legislation had been to ensure the prevention of poverty arising out of unemployment, sickness, widowhood, and old age, whereas the raising of income levels in employment had been left in the main to the bargaining of employers and trade unions. Irrespective of the methods employed to achieve these ends the fact is that the state had by now accepted a considerable degree of responsibility for the welfare—in the limited sense of ensuring a minimum physical standard of living—of its citizens. Not only was (and is) income secured, but within these national services provision was made for medical care.

Making available medical services through the Poor Law and the National Health Insurance scheme was an acknowledgement of the need to ensure that if services of this kind could not be bought out of income then they should be provided communally. The introduction of National Health Insurance was looked upon at the time as revolutionary, and from the comments made then one would have thought that this was the first attempt made by the state to provide services of a kind which the well-to-do were customarily able to buy for themselves out of income. Yet forty years earlier the same broad principles had been applied to education, and twenty years before the introduction of National Health Insurance in 1911 the principle of assisting in the provision of houses for the working classes had been accepted.

Without going into the details of all the legislation which was concerned with the needs of the poor and the working classes, or the fierce controversies which centred around the social reforms proposed and implemented in the first decade of the twentieth century,[1] it is quite clear that by the end of the First World War the state had assumed responsibilities and was carrying out functions designed to improve the welfare of those citizens, comprising a majority of the population, who were unable through inadequate income to pay for the services necessary for the achievement of a reasonable standard of life. The adequacy of the services made available, whether in the field of education, housing, medical care, or income maintenance, and the differences in the standards of the services collectively provided and those obtainable by the well-to-do through private purchase need not concern us at this point. What is important is the fact that by the 1920s we had become accustomed to talk of the provision of 'social services' by statutory authorities.

The use of the term social services in official reports dates from 1920 when the annual Treasury return (the Drage return) covering government expenditure on such services as public education, public health, old-age pensions, unemployment and health insurance, and poor relief was officially given the title of 'Annual return of expenditure on Public Social Services'.[2] Since then the term has gained currency and been applied so widely that 'no consistent principle seems to obtain in the definition of what is a social service'.[3] Nevertheless there are those who argue strongly that a welfare state is nothing more than one which provides social services, and the only dictionary definition of 'welfare state' which I have been able to find expressly defines a welfare state as 'one which has national health, insurance, and other social services'.[4] If the diligent reader, then, looks through the dictionary in order to find a definition or even a description of a social service he will be disappointed. Numerous meanings of 'social' and of 'services' are given, but the lexicographer through inadvertence or, more likely, inability does not provide a definition of the words 'a social service' or the 'social services' which have become part of our everyday language.

Some writers have attempted to give a specific meaning to these words. For example, J. J. Clarke has suggested that 'the social services are the services which a community provides for its own members, and to which the members of a community are entitled, to a greater or less degree, by reason of belonging to that community'.[5] The authors of a report published by Political and Economic Planning, an independent research group which carried out the one and only comprehensive review of the social services between the wars, defined them as 'a set of devices for providing people whose incomes are low or precarious, or both, with as many as possible of the essential facilities and resources which well-to-do families would naturally obtain in case of emergency'.[6] On the other hand the most recent and most widely approved major book on *The Social Services of Modern England* by the late M. Penelope Hall avoids a specific definition. However, in the introduction Miss Hall discusses 'the criteria by which the social services can be distinguished from other forms of public and voluntary effort contributing to the general good'.[7] The hall-mark of a social service, she argues, is that of direct concern with the personal well-being of the individual, and the basis is 'to be found in the obligation a person feels to help another in distress, which derives from the recognition that they are in some sense members one of another'. Modern developments, she believes, have widened considerably the scope of services which were originally directed at the needs of the poor, and by the middle of the twentieth century 'the state . . . has gradually assumed responsibility for meeting the basic needs of all its citizens . . . widening the scope of the social services to include the whole community, without distinction of social or economic class.'

One must, unfortunately, agree with Miss Hall that 'the terms "social service" and "the social services" are . . . sometimes used rather vaguely, and universal agreement has not yet been reached as to which services should be classified as social'.[8] But if they are an essential ingredient, or as some would argue the essence, of a welfare state we ought surely to make more positive attempts to clarify which of the myriad varieties of services in a modern complex society are social, and why and for what reasons we distinguish them.

In the past, services provided by the community through either voluntary or statutory organisations to relieve the poor could justifiably be distinguished as social services, but so too could services intended to maintain the living standards of the community as a whole, for example, public-health services, the police, public libraries, street lighting, roads, and public parks. If, however, we wish to isolate the social services as being different from other services publicly or socially provided, and it looks as though we do, then the criterion of direct concern with personal well-being would seem to be an adequate method of differentiation. Thus poor relief is always given to individual persons, and so too are medical care, education, unemployment benefit, an old-age pension, and the like, whereas street lighting, public parks, libraries, sanitation, water supplies and similar services are made available generally. It could be argued therefore that the social services are those provided by the community for no other reason than that of maintaining or improving individual well-being.

'For no other reason' is essential and is intended to distinguish these services from those which have aims other than the individual well-being of the recipients of the service. For example, commercial and industrial services of various kinds are provided under a capitalist system so as to benefit not only the recipients but also those who provide the service. There is the profit motive, and though in order to make a profit good quality services have (or ought) to be given to the recipients there is obviously the initial motive of benefit to the person providing the service. This simple truth was clearly recognised in the eighteenth century by the 'father' of British economic theory, Adam Smith, when he wrote 'Not from the benevolence of the butcher do we expect our dinner but from his regard for his own interest.'[9] We are not concerned with the ethics of the capitalist system, or the effectiveness of the profit motive as a means of raising living standards, but merely to show that in providing social services there is no thought of direct profit. There is (or ought to be) no other reason than that of ensuring individual well-being.

In recent years, especially since the end of the Second World War, the impression has been created that the social services are no longer directed at the particular needs of individuals, and in part this is due to the introduction of the concept of the universality of welfare provisions. The turning point marking the transfer of attention from the few to the many was probably the publication of the Beveridge Report in 1942. Hitherto the statutory social services had been limited to particular occupational and income groups, whereas the Beveridge proposals concerned all the adult population irrespective of occupation or income. For example, National Insurance against interruption or cessation of income was not henceforth to be confined to low-income or specified occupational groups, and a National Health Service was to be made available to everyone from the cradle to the grave. The emphasis on universality obscured the fact that even with these sweeping changes the benefits obtainable were still limited to persons having specified needs in times of specified contingencies, and therefore the basic principle of ensuring individual well-being was (and still is) applicable.

The belief that the aims and purposes of the social services had been completely revolutionised by the introduction of the concept of universality was further strengthened by the passing of the Family Allowances Act 1945. All parents having more than one child were to be given a standard allowance for each child by the state. Did this therefore mean the abandonment of the principle of need as a criterion for the provision of a social service?

Some would argue that it did, because even the wealthiest parents became entitled to family allowances, and of course millionaires are just as entitled to National Health medical services as the (financially) poorest members of the community. However, wealthy parents do not in fact receive as much as the less wealthy because family allowances are subject to income tax; and millionaires need not necessarily avail themselves of the service provided by the National Health Service. In any case, is there any real difference between giving a family allowance to parents whose income from employment does not take into account family responsibilities and the child allowance granted as a relief under the Finance Acts to income-taxpayers?[10]

There are by now infinite varieties of social provision which make the task of distinguishing the social services from other forms of social provision extremely difficult. There would seem to be no rational basis on which to make such distinctions, and Professor R. M. Titmuss has shown that the social divisions of welfare are far more complex and irrational than most people imagine. Yet many persist in believing that the social services are only for the poor or working classes (undefined) whose standards of living are raised by the generosity of taxpayers whose incomes are compulsorily reduced by the state so that the amounts taken by taxation can be redistributed among the recipients of the social services.

The idea that the social services are primarily a means of redistributing income from the rich to the poor is still commonly held, and it has been strongly argued that 'the essential marks of a social service are: (*a*) that it is rendered by, or on behalf of, the community to an individual or at most to a family, and appropriated to his or its exclusive use; and (*b*) that it contains an element of redistribution, i.e. that the majority of the individuals or families who avail themselves of it are receiving more than they give'.[11] It would be extremely difficult to prove that the majority receive more than they give, though it is probable that social provision is more economical than private provision and thus we all receive more than we give.[12] Even if there is an element of redistribution it is extremely doubtful if it is vertical, that is from the rich to the poor; but what is certain is that significant proportions of the expenditure on the social services are devoted to those who run and provide them and not only to those who receive them.

One of the outstanding features of the development of modern statutory social services has been the creation of vast administrative empires, well staffed and well paid, which constitute a powerful force in the pressure-group system of a democratic state. There is now a veritable army of civil servants and local government officers whose high standard of living depends on the perpetuation of the social services, and furthermore the way in which our taxation system has evolved into an elaborate, often incomprehensible, maze of direct and indirect taxes may well have resulted in the recipients of the social services paying themselves not only for their benefits but also for such things as agricultural subsidies and the expense accounts of businessmen.

We cannot measure adequately the precise ways in which incomes flow within and between groups, but it cannot be that in our society the social services are just gifts in the sack of the state Santa Claus which are distributed to the needy. Yet many critics have referred to modern Britain as a social service state, and some have even gone so far as to dub it a Santa Claus state, and implied in both these views is the notion that the state is merely distributing largesse to the many from the few. This is surely an unrealistic interpretation of what the social services are, what their purpose is, what their aims and functions ought to be, why they came into being and are still required. Whatever our views may be, the fact is that in mid-twentieth-century Britain we have an array of social services, statutory and voluntary, organised, financed, and administered in such a complex manner as almost to defy description.

We possess a variety of income-maintenance services such as national insurance, industrial injuries insurance, and supplementary benefits; an elaborate and comprehensive range of health services; services to promote and facilitate the finding of employment; various educational services; means of encouraging the building of houses to rent; a variety of services for 'special groups' such as the physically and mentally handicapped, offenders against the law, the aged, children deprived of a normal home life, and services to meet the needs of youth and to help the unborn child and its mother: services, in fact, to meet the needs of most people, from the cradle to the grave, or more graphically (and accurately), as the Americans would say, 'from womb to tomb'; and all financed and provided by the community as a whole and administered by public authorities and/or voluntary organisations.[13] Since 1948 there has been considerable expansion in the scope, the methods of organisation and administration, and the kinds of services provided, and above all in the resources of manpower and finance required to run them. The cost in labour and in money is in absolute terms considerably greater than ever before in our history, but whether the proportions of the national income and of the labour force devoted to them are unreasonably large is quite a different question.

There are some people who would like to see an even greater proportion of the national income allocated to, for example, the education and health services, but equally there are some who firmly believe that we are spending more than enough already and that more of the burden should be transferred from the community—the state—to the actual recipients of the services.[14]

In recent years there has been a tendency to concentrate discussion about these services on finance and all too rarely on the nature, the aims, and the value of them. What their value is to the community is not easily measured, but unless attempts are made to measure their contribution how can it be claimed that the expenditure of finance and effort is unjustifiably high or low? Those who deplore the growing burden of the social services appear to be interested only in their cost in terms of money and in relation to the total of state expenditure, and they rarely assess their value to the community. However, even in the 1960s out of the total of state (i.e. central government) expenditure nearly as much per £1 is spent on interest on the national debt and on the armed forces as is spent on the National Health Service, education, housing subsidies, the police, roads and agricultural subsidies put together. And in 1962 when the Government vigorously opposed an increase in pay for hospital nurses it had already granted substantial increases in pay to members of the armed forces. It may well be that in terms of social contribution a sergeant in the army is of more social worth than a sister in a hospital, and that in contemporary Britain we value more highly those who serve in the forces than those who tend the sick and injured. This of course we are fully entitled to do, but what then is our scale of values? Is expenditure on nuclear and conventional armaments deemed to be of more social worth than the prevention and cure of sickness? Is the ever-increasing cost of educational and health services to be deplored whereas the ever-increasing cost of armaments may be ignored?

These sorts of questions are all too rarely asked, but there is continuous questioning of the impact of the social services on government expenditure. In all discussions of the state of the nation and especially of the economic situation these services seem always, in recent years, to command extraordinary attention. One of the reasons for this remarkable interest is that many people assume that between 1945 and 1950 a revolution took place in the social services. Indeed there are those who believe that it is only since 1948[15] that we have had social services at all, whereas of course all that really occurred then was that at last some semblance of orderliness was introduced into a half-century's piecemeal development of haphazard social legislation. Nevertheless there is undoubtedly a general impression that in the years immediately following the Second World War Britain became a social service state. But is this necessarily a welfare state?

Just as most writers and politicians have avoided defining the social services so too have they neglected to tell us what they mean when they write or talk about the welfare state, and one is almost forced to the conclusion that in the main these words have very little real meaning. What is certain is that they have gained currency only very recently. It was during the Second World War and in the immediate post-war years, when there was a ferment of social legislation, that they became part of our everyday language. Looking back to the war years and the proposals then made for new kinds of social policies in the peaceful years to come, it is relatively easy to see why we needed a graphic term to indicate what society was to be like in the future.

As early as 1939, Sir Anthony Eden had argued in Parliament that war 'exposed weaknesses ruthlessly and brutally ... which called for revolutionary changes in the economic and social life of the country',[16] and Professor R. M. Titmuss in his admirable study of the development of the social services during the war has shown conclusively that:

by the end of the Second World War the Government had, through the agency of newly established or existing services, assumed and developed a measure of direct concern for the health and well-being of the population which, by contrast with the role of government in the nineteen-thirties, was little short of remarkable. No longer did concern rest on the belief that, in respect to many social needs, it was proper to assist the poor and those who were unable to pay for services of one kind and another. Indeed, it was increasingly regarded as a proper function or even obligation of government to ward off distress and strain not only among the poor but almost all classes of society. And, because the area of responsibility had so perceptibly widened, it was no longer thought sufficient to provide through various branches of social assistance a standard of service hitherto considered appropriate for those in receipt of poor relief—a standard inflexible in administration and attuned to a philosophy which regarded social distress as a mark of social incapacity.[17]

The war undoubtedly forced on us the realisation that a nation consists of living people all dependent on each other, and that the long-cherished assumptions concerning the superiority of some people compared with others, and the granting of privileges to the few and not the many, were untenable when the very existence of our society was at stake. From the beginning we were to be shown that this war was going to be very different from those fought in the past, and though it took us some time to realise that enemy bombs did not discriminate between dukes and dustmen, we were quickly forced to accept that the only way to survival was by the effort of the nation as a whole.

That all were engaged in war whereas only some were afflicted with poverty and disease had much to do with the less constraining, less discriminating scope and quality of the war-time social services. Damage to homes and injuries to persons were not less likely among the rich than the poor, and so, after the worst of the original defects in policy had been corrected—such as the belief that only the poor would need help when their homes were smashed—the assistance provided by the Government to counter the hazards of war carried little social discrimination and was offered to all groups in the community. The pooling of national resources and the sharing of risks were not always practicable nor always applied; but they were the guiding principles. Acceptance of these principles moved forward the goals of welfare.[18]

The threat of invasion in 1940 wrought a transformation in the attitudes of the rulers and the ruled towards society and in the way it should be (and had to be in war) organised. Professor Titmuss has suggested that:

the mood of the people changed and, in sympathetic response, values changed as well. If dangers were to be shared, then resources should also be shared. Dunkirk, and all that the name evokes, was an important event in the war time history of the social services. It summoned forth a note of self-criticism, of national introspection, and it set in motion ideas and talk of principles and plans. *The Times*, in a remarkable leader a few weeks after the evacuation of the British Expeditionary Forces from the Continent, gave expression to these views. 'If we speak of democracy, we do not mean a democracy which maintains the right to vote but forgets the right to work and the right to live. If we speak of freedom, we do not mean a rugged individualism which excludes social organisation and economic planning. If we speak of equality, we do not mean political equality nullified by social and economic privilege. If we speak of reconstruction, we think less of maximum production (though this too will be required) than of equitable distribution.' This was a declaration of faith, and these broad generalisations, subject as they will be to revision by historians better placed to study this phase of the war, are relevant to the story of welfare.[19]

And, surely, to the development of the principles and practices of the welfare state.

The story of what in fact happened during and after the war has been amply documented in legislation, government white papers, official reports, and many books, and our concern is with the extent to which social policy was so transformed as to justify the view that we became a welfare state.[20] We know that the social services were expanded and reorganized, but all too often they were still looked upon as an ambulance at the bottom of the cliff rather than a fence at the top to prevent persons falling over. Thus unemployment insurance, valuable as it is and has been, does not prevent unemployment, and if our society is to ensure the right to work we must, obviously, have a positive policy of employment.

One of the assumptions made by Lord Beveridge when he proposed a new system of social security was that there must be an employment policy, and two years later he argued cogently that the 'maintenance of employment is wanted for its own sake and not simply to make a plan for social security work more easily'.[21] The Coalition Government accepted this principle in 1944[22] and no government since then has repudiated it. We have therefore come to accept that the state has a duty to ensure that employment opportunities are made available, and implicit in this notion is the fact that unemployment is no longer regarded as simply the fault of the individual.[23] Since the well-being of an individual and of those dependent on him rests mainly on the income he earns from employment, the acceptance by the state of the obligation to ensure that as far as possible opportunities for employment are continuously made available is a clear indication that at long last a fundamental factor for the welfare of all citizens has become a communal responsibility. How to maintain full employment, the problems involved in and resulting from its maintenance, and the consequential effects on the economic, social, and political sytems are obviously all of great significance, but at this point we are concerned with only aims and not methods or achievements. If a state consciously and deliberately holds as one of its aims the maintenance of full employment then it is on the way to becoming a welfare state.

In modern developed industrialized societies the range of skills and knowledge necessary to perform the myriad varieties of jobs is enormous, and consequently the degree of education and training required by each worker varies substantially. Even to live at all in an advanced society necessitates education of a kind which cannot normally be provided individually by parents for their children, and for the past hundred years or so the state has accepted the responsibility of providing collectively for the formal education of children. Until 1944 it was only elementary education which was compulsory, and the opportunities for proceeding to 'higher education' were limited to the relatively few who could win scholarships (and those whose parents could afford to maintain them) and those who had the means of buying a grammar or public-school or university education. Under the Education Act 1944, the state has decreed that all children must be educated according to their age, aptitude, and ability, and the intention presumably is to eliminate inequalities in educational opportunities. If it is accepted that formal education contributes to individual and social well-being, apart from the obvious relationship between particular kinds of jobs and specialized education, then the aim of ensuring equality of educational opportunity by state action is surely one which would be found in a welfare state. The extent to which inequalities have been reduced in practice, and indeed whether it is practicable ever to achieve complete equality of educational opportunity, will be discussed later, but we have now a more elaborate and comprehensive system of education than ever before, collectively provided and presumably contributing to individual and collective well-being.

If a state consciously tries to ensure the maintenance of employment opportunities, and every child and young person has the chance of being educated so as to play its full part in the economic and social system, then at least it will have made a substantial contribution to the attainment of individual well-being. And if, in addition, it makes provision through a variety of social services for income maintenance at all times, and for the care of those who for one reason or another cannot provide for themselves, then it must be looked upon as being concerned with the welfare of its citizens. But more is needed to ensure the well-being of all its members. They need protection from actual or potential enemies; they need a system of defence against the members of their own society who engage in anti-social acts, whether in the form of physical assault, adulteration of foodstuffs, the sale of dangerous goods, a breach of contract for services rendered or promised, the domination of officials, or exploitation by employers; and perhaps above all they need safeguards to reduce the possibility of control of the state by an unscrupulous minority. Equally, they need collectively to protect themselves against the forces of nature, and though in this country we are not normally troubled by hurricanes typhoons, whirlwinds, earthquakes, droughts and locusts, there have on occasion been disastrous floods and freak winds which have seriously affected individual well-being.

We have built up elaborate defence systems against the various forces that threaten our daily lives. We have conventional and nuclear armaments and armed forces on a scale (and at a cost) which would have been looked upon as quite fantastic even thirty years ago; an elaborate system of criminal and civil law with machinery for its enforcement, and a growing number and variety of statutory tribunals; an impressive array of inspectors (who are presumably protectors) of Public Health, Weights and Measures, Factories, Shops, Mines, Explosives, Drugs, Gas, Electricity, Water, Fisheries, Agriculture, Taxes, Education, Customs and Excise, Slaughterhouses and Meat, Animals, of Children's and Probation departments, Fire Services, Constabulary, Housing and Planning, and a host of others too numerous to mention; and, of course, an intricate network of other forms of social control, some of which are clearly recognisable if not easily definable, which enables us to live in harmony with each other and with society.

There has been a tendency in recent years to regard society and the state as synonymous, and hence to consider the interests of the state as being entirely the same as those of society. This identification is quite misleading because the state is simply a form of organization; the people organised politically to fulfil specified functions, to exercise a measure of (but not complete) control over relationships within society, and to act as a means of contact between states. Even in the most highly developed state there are forms of conduct, types of associations, and informal relationships which have grown up within society and form part of its essential fabric over which the state has no control and, as long as individuals have even a limited freedom of choice, it never will be able to exercise control. And this is as it should be in a democratic state where limitations on individual freedom of action should be restricted only to those necessary for the maintenance of a stable system of social relationships and a just distribution of the resources required to maintain life.

The fact that in Britain the state now controls far more of the material resources of the nation, directs and influences their distribution to a greater degree than ever before, and imposes restraints on a far greater variety and number of forms of individual action than in the past, has given rise to the idea that our society is now completely dominated by the state. A moment's reflection, however, is sufficient to show that much of what we think, say, do, and want our lives to be as individuals or groups is under our own control, and so it should be. But we need to be ever vigilant against the encroachment by the state on more of our civil liberties than is required for the smooth running of society. The state should be the servant of society and not its master; and we should always recall that it is not an inanimate object but an organised body of people, public servants and politicians, who are themselves members of society elected or appointed to look after our best interests.

How the state can best serve the interests of society is (or ought to be) the fundamental question continuously asked by politicians and public servants.[24] In the past it was firmly believed that the 'good society' could best be achieved by the state interfering as little as possible in economic and social affairs. Now the most commonly held view seems to be that the state must of necessity effectively promote (and even control) economic activity and guide (and even direct) social affairs. In Britain today there are probably very few people, and certainly no major political groups, who publicly advocate that the coal, electricity, gas, and even railway industries should be taken out of the hands of the state; that the Post Office, the Bank of England, the B.B.C., B.O.A.C., Cable and Wireless Ltd., the state pubs in Carlisle, and the Crown Lands should be handed over to private enterprise; that the state should have no responsibility for roads, bridges, rivers, canals, sewerage, water supplies, the quality of foods and drugs, housing standards, air pollution, public health, working conditions, air, sea, road, and rail safety, the standards of books, films, plays, the protection of wild-life, the utilisation of land, and oversight of the economic activities of the nation; and that formal education, personal ill-health, income maintenance, and other contingencies should be purely the personal responsibility of the individual and his family and no concern of the state. Perhaps the ultimate decision in this country of exercising control over personal incomes and prices was the passing of the Prices and Incomes Act in 1966 which established a National Board for Prices and Incomes. Theoretically, at least, the state was now able to control prices and incomes though how effectively it has done so is still an open question.

There are, however, divisions of opinion as to the degree of responsibility which the state should accept and on the ways it should be fulfilled. For example, there are those who believe that the railways are an essential feature of an industrialized society and should therefore be run as a public service, that is they should be paid for wholly out of public funds without any direct charge to the user in the same way as roads are no longer paid for by tolls; on the other hand, there is a body of opinion which argues that the railways, even though state-owned and obviously essential, must operate on well-established commercial principles and so aim at making a profit by charging users fares and freight charges more than sufficient to cover the costs of operation. Similarly, though presumably with no commercial profit in view, there are those who advocate that public education and some branches of the National Health Service should be paid for by the users, whereas others argue that they should be provided socially free of direct cost to the user. These disagreements are substantially over means rather than ends, and there is a growing tendency to confuse ends and means and furthermore to differentiate some of the aims (or ends) of state activity as being concerned with welfare whereas the rest are not.

The well-being of all individuals in complex industrialised societies depends fundamentally on the economic system, on the success achieved in producing real wealth, and the way it is shared. Until very recently one of the main areas of disagreement between the major political parties concerned the extent to which the state should plan and control economic activity so as to ensure optimum economic growth and hence a continuously rising standard of living. The Labour Party was usually believed to be in favour of state planning and control of 'the commanding heights' of the economy, and when it was in power from 1945 to 1951 it was constantly accused of pursuing policies designed primarily to bring the whole economic system under the control of the state, and hence to exercise considerable control over the lives of individuals and their welfare. The Conservative Party, on the other hand, was usually looked upon as being in favour of encouraging economic growth through private enterprise with the minimum of state control and direction of economic affairs, and had a declared aim 'to set the people free', presumably from the clutches of the state.

When the Conservative Party came to power in 1951 many of its supporters undoubtedly hoped that some (if not all) of the measures of state planning and control introduced or substantially increased by the Labour Government would be drastically modified, and the word 'planning' would be erased from political discussion. Indeed 'planning' became, as political commentators have since noted, a 'dirty word'. However, by 1963, when the Conservative Party had been in office continuously for twelve years, the unbiased observer of the political scene would surely find difficulty in proving that the functions of government then were fundamentally different from what they had been in the years 1945–51. Almost all the nationalised industries were still in existence in substantially their original form; the structure, organisation, and functions of the social services had hardly changed at all; the control and regulation of economic activity by means of state budget policies and manipulation of the Bank Rate (with varying degrees of success) had been a major function of government; expenditure by the state (central and local governments) had continually increased so that the state in absolute terms spent more of the nation's income than ever before; the policy of subsidising out of public funds certain industries, especially agriculture, and amenities like houses, had not been abandoned; the aim of attempting to ensure full employment and a rising standard of living had been accepted even to the extent of appointing, in 1957, an expert committee—the Cohen Committee, familiarly known as 'the three wise men'—whose terms of reference were 'Having regard to the desirability of full employment and increasing standards of life based on expanding production and stability of prices, to keep under review changes in prices, productivity, and the level of incomes (including wages, salaries, and profits) and to report thereon from time to time'; and, finally, in 1961 the Conservative Government publicly acknowledged that the state has a responsibility to plan for economic growth when it introduced a deliberate policy of wage restraint, the so-called 'wages pause', and established a National Economic Development Council (Neddy). When the Labour Party succeeded in gaining a small majority in Parliament in 1964 and then a larger majority in 1966 and formed the Government, it firmly re-emphasised the need for state planning even to the extent of publishing a National Plan and setting up a Department of Economic Affairs and Regional Economic Planning Boards. Undoubtedly the Labour Government believed that planning by the state of social and economic affairs was essential to the development of the welfare state.

How far these planning measures were deliberately thought out and introduced because they were believed to be in the best interests of society, and how far they were simply the result of political expediency, remains to be seen, but it would appear as though 'planning' is no longer a 'dirty word'. It would seem, too, as if the necessity for state planning is no longer a major distinguishing feature of the main political parties, even though the instruments to be used and the emphases placed on the various factors which influence economic development may differ.

The acceptance of the need for planning is indicative of the part which the state now plays in influencing the economy and hence in the standard of well-being which can be achieved by society and its individual members. Economic planning is obviously directly concerned with welfare, and this simple truth has been recognised by the insistence of governments, during and since the Second World War, that the essential requirement for raising standards of living all round is a 'sound economy', and that so-called 'welfare services' can only be made available out of the economic efforts of the nation. To suggest, therefore, that a welfare state is one in which the social services are the main (or perhaps the only) concern of the state is to misrepresent what in fact has happened in Britain.

It might of course be argued that the state should only be concerned with the welfare (in a limited sense) of its members who for reasons beyond their own control do not receive an adequate share of the national wealth. Thus we might find a society whose economic effort produced more than sufficient for the needs of those engaged in actual production, but the non-producers, for example the sick and disabled, the aged and the unemployed, were not looked after. This could hardly be called a welfare society. If, however, the producers voluntarily set aside part of their rewards to succour the 'needy', or if the state compulsorily earmarked part of the wealth produced to distribute to the non-producers yet played no part in assisting the economic effort, it could presumably be called a welfare state.

The history of Britain over the past six or seven hundred years shows that the state has always played some part in the economic affairs of the nation; for example, as early as 1351 the Statute of Labourers introduced a form of state control of wages and prices; the Navigation Act 1381 was a deliberate attempt to protect the English shipping industry; and the imposition of import and export duties from the Norman conquest onwards was clearly an economic measure. State intervention in economic affairs is obviously not a twentieth-century invention, and the history of the past hundred years shows that, despite the efforts of philanthropists and charitable organisations to succour the needy, gross inequalities in wealth and income distribution could not be removed by voluntary effort.

The radical changes which have occurred in the past hundred years in, for example, the size and structure of our population, in the methods of production and exchange of wealth, in the growth of knowledge, in the concepts of democracy and of the rights of man,[25] have so transformed our society as to make it inconceivable that we could live together without the elaborate and complex organisation of the state. What its aims, purposes, and methods are will vary from one society to another, but we in this country claim by now to have evolved a welfare state which is, presumably, one in which there are conscious and deliberate policies for ensuring at least a minimum standard of life at all times for everyone, and, as far as possible, equality of opportunity for everyone to achieve the best out of life commensurate with aptitude and ability.[26]

If this is a fair assessment of what a welfare state is (or ought to be) then to what extent do we now have deliberate policies of these kinds? How do we attempt to implement them, and what degree of success do we achieve? These are fundamental questions which must be answered before we finally decide what the welfare state is in Britain in the second half of the twentieth century; and at the same time we may be in a position to judge how far we have succeeded in fulfilling the dreams of nineteenth-century social reformers like John Ruskin who less than a hundred years ago argued that 'I hold it for indisputable, that the first duty of state is to see that every child born therein shall be well housed, clothed, fed and educated till it attain years of discretion. But in order to the effecting of this the Government must have an authority over the people of which we now do not so much as dream' (*Time and Tide*, Letter XIII).

# The creation and implementation of social policies 2

The extent to which the state should direct and control the lives of individuals and the organisations they create has for centuries been a major theme of discussion for philosophers, and in more recent times for political scientists, economists, politicians, and even the 'man-in-the-street'. Many of the opinions and beliefs firmly held in the past have little relevance to contemporary Britain because our society today is so very different from that of even a century ago, and doubtless by the end of the twentieth century it will be quite different from what it is now. This does not mean that we should ignore all historical evidence and cast aside long-established proven principles, policies, and practices; but equally we should not place too much reliance on the past and assume that anything which has stood the test of time will necessarily do so for evermore. Tradition has its value, but it can also inhibit progress, and all too often in the development of social policy[1] any slight move forward has been made with extreme caution and on the basis of not departing too far from the traditionally accepted. Even those measures of social reform, introduced in the first half of the twentieth century, hailed in their days as 'social revolutions' seem on reflection to be far less revolutionary than was (and often still is) commonly supposed, and in any case most of them had already been in operation in other countries before being accepted here. The first principle of the evolution of the welfare state in Britain can, therefore, be enunciated: retrospection before social action; a commendably cautious principle in some circumstances, prosaically pragmatic in others, and based essentially on belief in the virtues of tradition.

Traditionalism does not encourage innovation, and looking back over the past century and a half to try to see the ways in which the concern of the state for the welfare of its citizens has changed we find, all too often, that it was by modification and not by innovation that reforms were made. Until the nineteenth century the state showed little concern for the well-being of the majority of its citizens, but there was of course a direct interest in making provision for the needs of the very poor. It could be argued that the Poor Laws constituted the first stage in the emergence of the welfare state, but whether or not this is its true origin, what is apparent is that many of the principles and practices used in the early Poor Laws have remained extant, and have to a considerable degree dominated our approach to the welfare measures of modern times.[2]

Originally the fundamental principle of poor relief was that the family should be responsible for the care of its poverty-stricken members: in effect the state enjoined the poor to look after the poor, an injunction which was as impracticable as that of expecting the blind to lead the blind. It soon became necessary, however, to place the responsibility on the community and this established the principle, which was henceforth to be enshrined, of the state delegating responsibility to localised communities. The poor, for example, had to be provided for by the other members of their parish, which at first glance seems reasonable and even socially just, but in fact inevitably resulted in inequalities and often injustice. Thus the burden of raising the finance required to provide support for the poorest was not equitably shared between the remaining members of the parish, and under the systems of local taxation used in the past to raise revenue it was impracticable to ensure an equitable distribution of that burden. Indeed it still is, and at long last it is being realised that the main method of raising revenue for local authorities in this country by a 'rate' levied on property is inequitable. The proportion of the 'poor rate' borne by those who were themselves only just above the poverty line was probably grossly excessive so that basically it was the less-poor who provided for the very poor. Inequities there must have been (as there still are) in the share of communal responsibility borne by each individual.

Not only was there an inequitable distribution among the less-poor and the well-to-do within the locality, but also between localities there were marked variations in the amounts of responsibility which had to be accepted in caring for the poor. In some areas the proportion of the population existing in conditions of dire poverty was very low, in others very high, and obviously the taxable capacities of areas differed significantly with the result that if a person were very poor the amount and kind of support he received depended on the area he lived in, and if he were not poor the amount of contribution he had to make depended on where he lived too: a paradoxical situation in a unified state. Yet even in the middle of the twentieth century the amounts and kinds of 'welfare' a person receives, and the share of the burden of providing 'welfare' borne by an individual, depend all too often on where he resides and not on individual need or personal ability to contribute.

This obsession with locality as the basic factor in determining policy was especially prominent in those spheres of state action directly concerned with individual well-being, and it is only very recently that a trend towards national as distinct from local policies and practices has been established.[3] This trend towards national as distinct from local responsibility for helping persons in need was tentatively introduced in 1908 when non-contributory old-age pensions based on a means test were provided by the state, and further strengthened by the introduction of National Insurance in 1911. The great depression of the inter-war years proved beyond any possibility of doubt that national policies were essential and above all the glaring inequalities which arose out of placing the burden for the relief of poverty on the locality and not the nation. When the incidence of unemployment and the financial burden of providing 'relief' became so heavy in some areas, as they did in the 1930s, that the locality could not possibly solve its own problems and the only possible solution lay in the acceptance by the state of a national responsibility, we entered a new phase in the development of welfare policies.

The recognition of 'depressed areas' and the establishment of a national system of unemployment assistance in 1934 constitute a major departure from the principle of dependence on the locality for the maintenance of a minimum standard of life. In 1948 (with the passing of the National Assistance Act) the principle was firmly established that the relief of financial poverty was the responsibility of the state, and that any citizen on proof of 'need' was entitled to receive from public funds an income sufficient to provide a minimum level of subsistence. The fundamental problems involved in applying these principles are those of determining 'need' and the level of subsistence. Basically we all need a minimum of food, clothing, and shelter to maintain life, and in an economic system which uses money as a means of exchange and a measure of value it is necessary to express the minimum in terms of money. Superficially it would appear to be a simple task to calculate how many shillings or pounds are required at a given time to ensure a minimum level of subsistence but in economically developed societies, where average standards of living have been continually rising and where yesterday's luxuries and comforts for the few become today's necessities for the many, this superficially simple task turns out to be exceedingly complex.[4]

In a primitive economically under-developed society a bowl of rice, or a handful of maize, a loin cloth, some water, and a mud hut may be sufficient to maintain life for an adult, but that same adult would not survive for long on that diet, clothing, and shelter in modern Britain. Some of course do exist, even in the Britain of the 1960s, on what would be for most of us a very inadequate means of subsistence. For example, those people designated in the National Assistance Act as 'persons without a settled way of living' (previously known as vagrants, vagabonds, wayfarers, tramps, dossers, and casuals) are restricted, in reception centres, to a rather limited diet, but this scale of subsistence is officially prescribed and presumably it is assumed that it represents the absolute minimum for those whose standards of living are very different from, and much lower than, those of the population in general.

Above this level are the National Assistance scale rates applicable to persons deemed to be in need, and these have varied from £2 per week (excluding a rent allowance) for a husband and wife in 1948 to £3 3s. in 1955, £4 5s. in 1959, £4 15s. 6d. in 1962, £5 4s. 6d. in 1963 and since 1966 Supplementary Benefit Rates which in 1969 were £7 17s. od. Were these incomes adequate to provide a standard of living compatible with human decency in what we have called during those years 'the affluent society'?

There is evidence, for example, from surveys made of the living conditions of old people, widows, and handicapped persons, which proves that many decent, respectable, worthy citizens who through no fault of their own had to rely on this sole source of income found life extremely difficult. See, for example, the surveys made by the then Ministry of Pensions and National Insurance into 'The Financial and other Circumstances of Retirement Pensioners' published by H.M.S.O. in 1966, and the Ministry of Social Security survey into the 'Circumstances of Families' published by H.M.S.O. in 1967. Even ordinary observation would lead those of us who are more fortunate to the view that it must be extremely difficult to achieve a reasonable standard of living on incomes of this order, and certainly it could be nowhere near the standard attainable by that often quoted but rarely identified character—the average wage-earner. Poverty is, of course, relative—if it were absolute then the drawing of a poverty line would be comparatively easy—and it is this difficulty of knowing where and for what reasons to draw the line which presents one of the most significant problems for the welfare state today.

B. Seebohm Rowntree showed us at the end of the nineteenth century how and in what ways to draw a poverty line, and made a most useful distinction between primary and secondary poverty.[5] Other social statisticians and Rowntree himself in the first half of the twentieth century were able, by means of social surveys, to show how changing social conditions required revisions of the datum over time, but the intractable problems of determining what the concept of poverty means and the innumerable difficulties of its measurements are still unresolved, not only in this country but in even more affluent countries such as the United States of America. One would have thought that in this predominantly scientific age we would by now be nearer to a real understanding of these problems than ever before, and that in our advanced stage of political, economic, and social development social policies designed to alleviate the effects of poverty would be based on a more systematic knowledge of when and in what circumstances a person can justifiably be termed poor than is the case at present.

It is not only the problems of definition of poverty or the determination of needs which create difficulty; there is the question of the allocation of resources. What proportion of the national income should be devoted to the alleviation and, preferably, eradication of poverty? Who knows; but what is clear is that much of our social policy is bedevilled by an apparent failure to determine priorities in relation to the allocation of resources of personnel and finance. The number of competing claims on the national purse has, of course, grown significantly as a result of the development of welfare policies, so that, for example, it becomes increasingly difficult to make decisions about whether to allocate more resources to, say, the health services and less to the education services, or more to child care services and less to old people's welfare, or more to building houses and less to the construction of factories and so on almost indefinitely. Indeed, if we consider the whole field of the state's economic and social policies, the myriad varieties of competing and complementary claims are beyond the comprehension of any one person.

The determination of priorities is clearly a fundamental problem, and in the past it was made even more intractable by the absence of systematic planning even within generally accepted fields of social policy. For example, the scourge of poverty arising from mass unemployment in the depression of the 1930s was not tackled by any systematic planning on a national scale, and it was not until 1942 when the Beveridge Report was published that an attempt was made to plan policies and services to prevent mass unemployment and poverty of that kind in the future.[6] Looking back it seems odd that a society which was even then highly industrialised and relatively wealthy was incapable of dealing more effectively with those economic and social problems, but, of course, many other countries were just as ineffective as we were, and perhaps one of the reasons for these failures was that it was not until the late 1930s that new ways of thinking about economic policies were developed. The publication, in 1936, of *The General Theory of Employment, Interest and Money* by J. M. Keynes, which was concerned in the main with 'a study of the forces which determine changes in the scale of output and employment as a whole', undoubtedly led in due course to a rethinking of traditional economic theory and its application to economic policy, and to what has since been called the 'Keynesian revolution'. However, it is difficult to isolate the individual factors which led us during the war years and especially in the years immediately following the second war to a very different concept of the role of the state and to a supposedly general belief that a welfare state is desirable, and maybe even essential and inevitable.

There is no doubt that after the war we created social policies designed to give the citizen 'rights' of a kind very different from those of the past;[7] but were we equally radical in finding the means of implementing those policies? The implementation of social and economic policies can only be carried out by people working in administrative organisations of various kinds,[8] and in this country we have traditionally used central government departments, sometimes specially created National Boards (for example, the Unemployment Assistance Board established in 1934 and later renamed the National Assistance Board in 1948), and, of course, locally elected councils under the system of local government created in the 1890s. We need not be concerned with the varieties of methods used in the past, but it is important to look at what happened in the period 1946–48.

For some of our new policies we established a national system of implementation; for example, to administer the new system of National Insurance introduced in 1948 we created a new Ministry of National Insurance to take over functions previously performed by a number of ministries,[9] and for the National Health Service we created Regional Hospital Boards to administer hospital services. But for the Health Service we also used local authorities to administer much of our public health services and of course we created Executive Councils to administer the general practitioner, pharmaceutical and dental services. This so-called tripartite division of administration was, to say the least, cumbersome even though novel,[10] but for many of the other services we obeyed the traditional pattern of handing over national policy to be implemented by local authorities. So that, for example, the public health services were to be administered by local health authorities which varied enormously in size of population, in resources, and in their willingness and ability to incur expenditure. There were then 146 such authorities in England and Wales and an intelligent observer from abroad might well be justified in asking why this number of administrative units was necessary in such a relatively small country. He could of course have equally well have asked why educational services had to be provided by local authorities, and why even as late as 1968 we needed 174 children's departments to provide child care services under the Children's Act of 1948 and subsequent amendments.

The answer to that question would usually be that services of this kind are essentially local and therefore are best provided and controlled by locally elected representatives and locally appointed officials. This may, of course, be true, but what proof have we that it is, and in any case does the process of child-bearing differ from one locality to another? If this belief in the virtues of local government was carried to its logical conclusion, ought we to insist that elected representatives must have been born and bred in the locality, that all those who actually provide the services must be locals, and that only local inhabitants are entitled to receive the services? In practice there is a strong tendency in some areas to favour the 'local man' for appointment to local government service irrespective of the quality of applicants from 'outside', and there are still traces of the application of the principles of the seventeenth-century Laws of Settlement (originally intended to restrict the movement of paupers from one parish to another) to citizens applying for services in an area in which they are not normally resident. For example, an unmarried mother-to-be may, for obvious reasons, wish to have her confinement in an area away from that in which she normally resides, but she may find difficulty in obtaining the services decreed by the state as hers by right of citizenship.

The greater part of the services concerned with the maintenance of health is not under the control of locally elected authorities and is administered either regionally or in effect nationally. For example, the medical services provided by general practitioners are administered by 138 appointed Executive Councils, and a citizen normally resident in London and having an illness whilst on a visit to Wigan would not be debarred from obtaining these services when away from home; hospital services of various kinds are administered by fourteen Regional Hospital Boards appointed by the Minister of Health and a citizen normally resident in one region who suffers an illness or accident when on a visit to another region would not be denied hospital treatment. However, the intelligent citizen may still be wondering why such a variety of organisations is necessary to ensure the provision through the state of a comprehensive national health service, and is surely justified in asking if it would not have been more rational to have created, in 1948, fourteen regional all-purpose health authorities under the control of the Minister of Health.

A system of regionally administered health services would obviously be less cumbersome, complex, and fragmentary than that which now exists, and in allied fields of social services, for example national insurance and assistance, the regional principle of administration has been adopted. The main objections to its adoption for the administration of all the health services were, presumably, the loss of local democratic control, the fear that regional authorities would become vast impersonal machines inappropriate for the provision of essentially personal services, and that the Ministry of Health would become all-powerful.

These dangers may be real, but they have not been eliminated by the existing tripartite system of organisation; and underlying such fears and objections there are obviously a number of assumptions which are, as yet, nothing more than assumptions. Are we fully entitled to assume that local democratic control by elected representatives is so vital, valuable, and more effective than any other form of control? If so, we must assume that local councillors are genuinely representative of the local population, and that their selection and subsequent election is truly democratic. Furthermore, we have to assume that the sole aim of the elected member is to look after the interests of the community, and that he will always act with widsom and exercise sound and independent judgement in pursuit of that aim. Admirable assumptions, but in reality we do not know whether elected members are truly representative, or whether their sole aim is to serve the best interests of the community.

The selection of candidates to stand for local authority elections is a mysterious, secretive, and weird process, and not always democratic; the growing emphasis on 'party power politics' in local government results all too often in members following the party line even if it conflicts with the known wishes of the electors; usually the successful candidate is elected only by a minority of the voters; and above all else what real power does the elected member have to mould and control the services of the authority, and what special qualities does he possess to exercise such responsibilities as are placed upon him?

The trend since 1948 has been to transfer ultimate control to the central government departments while lip-service is paid to the major role still left to local government in the running of the country. For example, the duties of local health authorities are clearly laid down in Acts of Parliament, their functions and responsibilities formally defined, and approval of the Minister is often necessary for decisions involving relatively modest items of expenditure, so that, incidentally, the powers of the Ministry are probably neither more nor less than they would be with a regional system. However, the crucial question which must be asked about the system of local government administration is: can the elected lay member be expected to know and understand the technicalities of the organisation he is assumed to control in these days of specialised legislation and highly specialised services?

It would be illuminating to know how many councillors sitting on health committees have read (and understood) the numerous Acts and statutory regulations relevant to their functions, and how many keep abreast of the ever-growing flood of circulars intended to ensure the progressive (and on occasion retrogressive) development of the service? Even the most conscientious member must find difficulty in devoting to his spare-time duties the time required to keep up to date with the information essential for the adequate fulfilment of his duties. Many intelligent, sincere, and worthy members admit that finding time to read all the mass of papers sent to them before every meeting is itself a problem. How can any human being doing a full-time job for five days a week, and playing his part as a member of a family, find sufficient time to digest the mass of information which must of necessity be read and understood if he is to contribute to the reasoned discussion which should precede the making of any policy decision? The demands on the time of every person deemed to be giving 'public service' are extraordinarily heavy and varied; there are meetings and conferences to attend, political contacts to be maintained, and a readiness to be at the beck and call of all kinds of individuals and organisations must always be shown. The day is only of twenty-four hours' duration, and the week has only seven days in it for councillors as for the rest of us; it is therefore not surprising to find that it is becoming increasingly difficult to recruit candidates for local government elections from the younger sections of the population. The problem of finding sufficient time could be solved by restricting the membership of councils to the retired or person of independent means, or by making it into a full-time paid job, but this would hardly be democratic nor would it necessarily ensure that the members were sufficiently capable of understanding the knowledge required to fulfil their duties.

The outstanding example in recent years of the burden of knowledge imposed on county and county borough councillors was in 1948 when they were presented with a mass of papers detailing the future functions of the authorities as determined by Parliament in the immedate post-war years. Vitally important decisions had to be made affecting the well-being of millions of citizens, appointments of new chief officers and the establishments of their departments had to be settled, committees had to be formed, and in effect that part of the structure of the welfare state deemed appropriate for provision by local authorities had to be created.

What, in practice as distinct from theory, was the nature of the discussions and deliberations in most local authorities at that time? Are we to assume that in every county and county borough council all the councillors knew what all this legislation was about, that membership of the appropriate committees was decided on a rational basis, that selection committees knew the type of person and the qualities to be looked for when making the new appointments arising out of the statutes, and that the elected members (and indeed the existing chief officers) appreciated fully the need for an approach and attitude under the new legislation which would be different from those prevalent in the day of the Poor Law? No one person can know what the situation was in every authority, but from discussions with some members of a few county and county borough councils at that time, and from a limited research study into the implementation of one of the new Acts carried out in 1956, the impression gained is that elected representatives relied heavily on summaries provided by the Clerk and technical advice given by the Medical Officer of Health. If this was the general practice then the part played by councillors in framing policy and shaping the structure of the new systems was not very significant. This is not to suggest that elected members failed in their duty or that the paid officials exceeded their duty; it is simply an attempt to assess realistically the extent to which national social policy can be implemented by spare-time, locally elected councillors.

Systematic studies of the role of elected members in framing, making, and shaping social policy, having oversight of its implementation, and assessing its results are all too rare, so that the protagonists of the existing system of local government can (and do) make claims for the great contribution made to the well-being of the individual and society with impunity. Systematic studies may reveal that these claims are grossly exaggerated, and in any case the apparent discontent in many areas with 'them on the Council' and the continued apathy of local government electors as evidenced by the low percentages of the poll at municipal elections, are in themselves indicative of the need to examine whether the system created in the late nineteenth century is appropriate for the radically changed social situation of the late twentieth century. And in such an examination an attempt should be made to determine whether an elected is necessarily more effective than an appointed authority; whether in an elective system the members really exercise control or are no more than a sounding board for paid officials; and above all whether

33

elections are so essential for the maintenance of democracy as to justify the inevitable inequalities in services from one part of the country to another.

Obvious inequalities abound under the existing system, and it is surely paradoxical that in a welfare state the quality of services which society decrees should be available as a right of citizenship can vary from excellent to barely adequate, depending on where one resides. Where the citizens on one side of a street have readily available the services of, for example, midwives, health visitors, home helps, and the like, whereas their neighbours across the road, because they happen to be under the jurisdiction of a different authority, have the greatest difficulty in obtaining such services, then the situation is not only paradoxical, it is unequivocally socially unjust.

The factors contributing to these inequalities may, on occasion, lie outside the control of the local authorities—for example, a genuine national shortage of midwives or home helps; or there may be a sincere failure to appreciate the 'needs' of the area and a mistaken assessment of the adequacy of the services in relation to the 'needs'; but more commonly the variations in availability and quality of services are due to the attitudes of elected members, their officials, and the taxable capacity of each area. Every member has the unenviable task of reconciling in his own mind a number of conflicting interests, and (it is to be hoped) the most difficult is that of wanting to provide the best possible services and at the same time keeping the burden on the ratepayers as light as possible. Reconciling the interests of the citizen, on the one hand as a ratepayer and on the other as a possible recipient of the services provided by the authority, may be an impossible task, but what is certain is that while there are such extraordinary variations in the taxable capacities of each area there are bound to be marked differences in the range and quality of services of all kinds capable of being provided. The central government has attempted to meet this proplem by means of 'equalisation grants' based on average rateable values, and since 1959 a general grant based on weighted populations, but these expedients serve only to emphasise the inequalities of local taxable capacities. In 1963 the so-called 'revolt over the rates' as a result of the revaluation of properties on current values once again made obvious the ludicrous nature of local rates as a method of raising revenue to finance essential services. Yet oddly enough instead of discussing the fundamental problems of whether local revenue raising on this basis is compatible with the aims of a welfare state, the apologists of local democracy have been concerned mainly with finding ways and means of shifting the financial burden from local authorities to the central government while apparently hoping to retain local control.

Apart from the problems of finance there are other serious issues. Thus, under our methods of local implementation how can we ever be certain that national social policy will always faithfully be carried through by local authorities? There are degrees of compliance, and where it is difficult to lay down objective standards of performance how can assessments be made of the extent to which the policies are being implemented? Where local authorities must provide a certain kind of service, tests can be applied to ensure that they do so, but the power of central over local government is not always as specific. In many fields of social policy the central authority does not insist, it merely exhorts or requests, and in these days of party politics, in local as well as central government, exhortation by, say, a Conservative government is likely to be heeded less by a solidly Labour council than one which is Conservative. If political affiliations are likely to be a determining factor in the ways and extent to which social policy is implemented then the kinds and quality of local services will vary from one authority to another. The provision of impersonal services deemed to be essential to life, such as coal, gas, and electricity supplies, have been deliberately removed from the political arena, and there is no suggestion that they should be returned to private enterprise or to local authorities. However, there is still the anomaly that an even more vital factor in maintaining life, water, is not nationally provided, despite the aims of the Water Act 1945 which gave the Minister of Health (and since 1951 the Minister of Housing) powers to implement a national water policy. No doubt in the near future we shall be forced to ensure water supplies on a national basis, but will we then accept that other services directed at the right to live are also nationally provided so as to guarantee equality of availability and quality?

Patterns of control in the future are a matter for conjecture,[11] but any proposals to reorganise radically, say, local health authorities will depend for their success on the power of local authorities to preserve their existing functions and anachronistic boundaries. There is still a strong belief among councillors, though not, one suspects, among the population at large, that local administration through elected members is the only and the best method. At the annual conferences of the two major national associations of local authorities, the Association of Municipal Corporations and the County Councils Association, strong emotional appeals are often made for services to be handed back to the local authorities. Demands have been made for transferring the hospital services from the control of the appointed Hospital Boards and Management Committees to the major local authorities, but it has yet to be proved they could in fact make a better job of running the hospitals than the appointed Boards. *Prima facie* there is every indication that if the responsibility for providing hospital services were handed over to county and county borough councils then the inhabitants of many areas could not expect to receive the range and quality of services now available to them. This is not to say that the Regional Hospital Board system is perfect, but the fact remains that areas of small population and low rateable values would find extreme difficulty in providing the specialised and costly services deemed to be necessary in the present advanced stage of medical knowledge and surgical skills. Furthermore, if, as seems to be suggested by the 'rate revolt' of 1963, local authorities are already finding the burden of meeting the costs of education to be too great then how could they possibly hope to find the means of financing hospital services?

The right of a local authority to continue in being may, in a democracy, be as important as the right to live of an individual human being, and from the spirited fight waged by some authorities in response to the proposals of the Local Government Commission[12] that they should no longer exist as administrative units there would appear to be, on the part of elected members and their officials, a firm belief in their right to continue to exist in an unchanged form for evermore. The motives of the elected members in resisting change are difficult to perceive; a cynic might suspect that some substantial material gain is obtained by being a member of a local council, or that there is in the heart of every councillor a love of power which can be satisfied by the assumed authority exercised by councillors over officials and the electors; or, at a higher level, the desire to preserve a local authority may be due to the altruistic belief that the best interests of the area can only be served by locals with intimate knowledge of and a genuine love for the locality. The motives of the officials are obvious. Extinction of the authority as an employing unit will necessitate the search for a new job, and the chances of obtaining a job of comparable status, security, and rewards in other fields of employment are not very bright. But they have secured for themselves conditions of compensation in the event of redundancy which are by no means ungenerous and certainly better than in most occupations.

A variety of reasons can be adduced for the continuance of local authorities as administrative units for the implementation of national social policies, and for the strength of the resistance on the part of elected members and their employees to proposals for rationalising areas; but in a welfare state is it possible to justify the retention of a system which inevitably leads to inequalities in the provision of services which in principle are deemed to be the right of every citizen? Undoubtedly the system has contributed substantially to the well-being of individuals and society as a whole in the past eighty odd years, not only materially but in less tangible ways, for example, by providing opportunities to practise the art of government by discussion, for individuals to serve their fellow men through public service and to spread knowledge of the principles, practices, and problems of democratic government. For these and many other benefits society as a whole should be grateful, but times have changed, knowledge in all fields is vastly greater than ever before, relationships between individuals and social classes are looked upon quite differently from what they were, and it is no longer assumed that to be born of humble parents or in some back street is a bar to the attainment of the rights and benefits, and the fulfilment of the obligations and duties, of citizenship. If equal opportunities are to be made available throughout the country for all citizens to share in the facilities and services which society decrees are to be provided out of the resources of the nation as a right of citizenship, and not on the basis of a residential or other discriminatory qualification, then obviously the existing system of local government must be radically changed.[13]

There are now indications of a move away from the use of anachronistic units of local government. For example, in 1968 the Government issued a Green Paper on the administrative structure of the medical and related services in England and Wales[14] in which it is suggested that the health services should be administered by a single authority in each area and that these area authorities should replace and undertake the functions now carried out by a large number of bodies, so that at long last, too, it has been suggested that local authorities should no longer have a multiplicity of 'social service departments' but should instead have a 'Social Work Department' as recommended by the Seebohm Committee. This has in fact already been implemented in Scotland by the Social Work (Scotland) Act 1968. We seem, therefore, to be moving away from the extraordinary maze of administrative units we used in the past towards a more co-ordinated system of national policies being implemented nationally which one would have thought was essential in a welfare state; but one must still ask the question: what is it that a welfare state really aims to do?

# Fulfilling the basic aims of a welfare state 3

In looking at welfare states throughout the world it seems that there are at least some common basic aims. If, for example, one looks at the Scandinavian countries, or New Zealand, Australia, or Britain, then it seems as though they all attempt (*a*) to ensure the maintenance of employment so as to guarantee the right to live for most of us; (*b*) to ensure the maintenance of a minimum income at all times; (*c*) to ensure the right to learn; and (*d*) the right to protection and community support when one is incapacitated physically or mentally.

It is, of course, only relatively recently that in this country we have come to accept that a policy of full employment is desirable not only for society as a whole but for every individual. The mass unemployment of the inter-war years and the degrading effects on an individual suffering long term unemployment through no fault of his or her own have at last been recognised as evils which a civilised society should not tolerate. The majority of people in most societies prefer, one suspects, to work for their living rather than be idle, but it is by no means easy to ensure that at all times there is work for everyone.

There is, perhaps, no practicable method in a free society of ensuring an even flow of the right people into the right jobs, or of maintaining a balance between the socially necessary, the socially desirable, and the less essential forms of employment. To decide objectively the value to the community of a particular job is an exceedingly difficult and complex task, but it is practicable, surely, to minimise the glaring differences in conditions of employment which in the past were based on the assumption that one kind of job was much more worthwhile than another. Why, for example, was the dustman (a vitally important person in densely populated areas) expected to work longer hours, have fewer holidays, and receive far less pay than the Town Clerk whose responsibilities in real terms would be difficult to assess? Failure to collect refuse could lead to the spread of disease; failure to keep the affairs of a council running smoothly may be highly inconvenient but not disastrous. Attitudes towards the real value of different kinds of jobs have changed markedly in recent years, and there has been a substantial reduction in the gap between the good conditions of employment for the few and the bad for the many; but greater equality in working conditions has not necessarily been accompanied by the removal of incomprehensible inequalities in remuneration, in conditions of service and security of tenure. Why should the hard-working, conscientious, skilled manual worker, who may have given thirty years of excellent service to one firm, be declared redundant and dismissed at one week's notice, whereas a director who may only have been with the firm three years is given a 'golden', or at least a 'silver', handshake and, because of the contacts made in that time, may be offered a directorship by another firm? Why should a school teacher, a university teacher, a civil servant and local government officer, and many others be guaranteed employment for their working lives, whereas an agricultural labourer, a dock worker, and a factory operative may be dismissed, or declared redundant, at perhaps one week's notice. Why indeed! And it is significant that in the House of Commons on 26 July 1962 the Prime Minister announced that the Government proposed to examine ways and means of giving greater security of tenure of employment to weekly-paid employees. There were, of course, 'good firms' which provided security of tenure and had schemes providing compensation in the event of redundancy for all classes of employee. It was not, however, until 1965 that a statutory system of redundancy payments for persons continuously employed for two years or more was introduced by the Redundancy Payments Act 1965.[1] This Act at least removes one of the obvious inequalities of the past, and with the additional measures adopted in recent years of attempting to create wider employment opportunities we may now be moving towards employment policies which will, in due course, give reality to the aim of equality of opportunity in employment.

But even if we succeed in achieving a realistic policy of full employment we may yet, even in a welfare state, have problems connected with the individual who prefers not to work for a variety of reasons. Fortunately the numbers and proportions of the real work-shy are very small, but we have still not resolved what should be done with persons of this kind other than send them to prison, which is hardly the most constructive way of dealing with them. If we succeed in achieving a real policy of full and constructive employment then perhaps we will need in the future to give far more thought to dealing with this minority group.

Much has clearly been achieved in abolishing the mass unemployment of the past and in creating a constructive policy of employment, and allied to these problems are those of the maintenance of income.

During the past fifty years the state in Britain has made deliberate plans designed to guarantee income in periods of interruption or cessation of individual earnings. The creation of the system of National Insurance in 1911 and of the safety net of Unemployment Assistance in 1934 (National Assistance in 1948 and Supplementary Benefits since 1966) has undoubtedly transformed the prospects of continued existence for the ordinary working man and reduced substantially one of the major fears of life for previous generations. Disputes there may well be about the levels of rates of benefit and assistance at any given point in time, but the fact remains that there is now a minimum of weekly income below which no one need fall provided either by right of being a qualified contributor or simply on grounds of citizenship and proof of need. A remarkable achievement in a relatively short period of time, but are the policies and practices consonant with the principles?

The basic principle of the system of national insurance is that benefits are provided to meet specified contingencies such as sickness, unemployment, old age, and widowhood, by virtue of contributions paid over specified periods of time. The theory is that by making virtually all adults regular contributors and calculating actuarially the contributions required from insured persons, their employers, and the state, a fund is established sufficient to meet the demands likely to be made arising out of interruption or cessation of earnings.

Hence there is in effect a system of national pooled savings designed to meet our individual needs in times of personal hardship, which most of us could not surmount ourselves. An admirable principle, theoretically sound, and hopelessly confused in its application.

The confusion arises out of the assumed virtues of the so-called contributory principle. This was best expressed in the Beveridge Report where it was dogmatically claimed that in a national scheme of social security what the British people desired was 'benefit in return for contributions'. Apparently we, as individuals, believed that if we (as employed persons) paid 9d. a week (as we did in the inter-war years) or 15s. 8d. a week (as we did in 1967) then we had earned the right to benefits at the appropriate rates when circumstances arose which made us qualified to receive benefit. And this is what we have been encouraged to believe ever since 1911, despite the fact that in the inter-war years the Unemployment Insurance Fund was heavily in debt, and that since 1948 no retirement pensioner can possibly have contributed enough to justify the relatively meagre retirement pension paid out of the National Insurance Fund. So that in practice the contributory principle has certainly not always been applied and it has become essentially an administrative device for determining entitlement to benefit on the basis of the number of contributions made and not their value.

Establishing the right to benefit in return for contributions in 1911, and maintaining the façade of insurance in the inter-war years, had many virtues, not the least being that the maintenance of income through the Unemployment and Health Insurance systems was clearly seen to be very different from the grudging assistance granted under the Poor Laws and from 1934 the Unemployment Assistance Acts. In those years the greater part of the adult population and certainly of insured persons did not qualify to pay direct taxes (notably income tax) though they were substantial payers of indirect taxes. Insurance benefits were therefore believed to have been earned, whereas Poor Relief and Unemployment Assistance were looked upon as state charity.

The dramatic change in the scale of taxation required to pay for the Second World War completely altered the situation in that nearly every employed adult became liable to pay income tax, and the introduction of the Pay As You Earn system in 1943 was a positive recognition of the fact that most of us had become direct contributors to the funds of the state. Henceforth, though this could not easily have been foreseen by Lord Beveridge when he made his analysis of the social insurance and allied services in 1942, the privilege of paying income tax was to be imposed on the many and not just the few; the distinction between the many who in the inter-war years paid National Insurance contributions but not income tax and the few who paid income tax but not National Insurance contributions virtually disappeared. Why, therefore, did we persist in maintaining a separate system of contributions to National Insurance when we were all in a variety of other ways contributors to the funds of the state?

Belief in the assumed virtues of benefit in return for contributions; an assumption that the discipline of paying a specified contribution is good for us; traditionalism on the part of policy-makers who having been steeped in the system for thirty years must have believed that it could continue for ever; and the commonly held belief among the public at large that National Insurance really did work on insurance principles were all contributing factors in the re-establishment on an extended scale, though with few substantive alterations, of the 'new' system of National Insurance in 1948.

If, as one assumes, the object was to ensure the maintenance of income during periods of interruption or cessation of earnings, what justification was there for paying a flat rate of benefit irrespective of the income the benefit was intended to replace? Equally what was the justification for flat-rate contributions when, presumably, the basic idea was to pool the contributions of persons having quite different capacities to contribute? And, above all, what was the point of having an enormously complex and costly administrative machine whose main function was to maintain contribution records and decide entitlement to benefit, when if, as a result of this costly process of decision-making, it was found that Joe Bloggs was not qualified for a benefit under the National Insurance Acts all he had to do was to make application to the National Assistance Board, from whom he would have received in all probability a higher rate of assistance than he would have received in benefit from the National Insurance Fund?

Surely even in the 1950s the time had come to re-examine the fundamental aims, principles, policies, and practices of National Insurance and the other related measures, that is National Assistance, Industrial Injuries Insurance, Family Allowances, and War Pensions, which together comprised our system of so-called social security, in the light of conditions prevailing in the affluent society of the second half of the twentieth century, rather than to continue to operate schemes designed to remove the gross inequalities of the nineteenth century and to combat (not very effectively) the depressed conditions of the 1920s and 1930s. The Labour Party made an attempt in 1957 to formulate a plan for 'half-pay on retirement'; but though retirement pensions impose the heaviest financial burden they are not the sole object of a system of social security. And the Conservative Government in 1959 made a slight breach in the seemingly impregnable wall of flat rate benefits and contributions by its introduction of a limited graduated retirement pension scheme.[2] In 1963 the Labour Party presented us with a plan of 'New Frontiers for Social Security', which at least recognised that making alterations in one part of a highly complex structure will not necessarily remedy the deficiencies and inconsistencies of the whole, and that 'the time is overdue for the whole scheme to be reconstructed', but 'on the old foundations', which may well mean a perpetuation of the existing inconsistencies which cannot easily be justified on rational grounds.

Why, for example, do we insist on the fulfilment of contribution conditions before granting a sickness benefit under National Insurance, whereas if the sickness can be shown to be due to an industrial accident or industrial disease contribution conditions do not have to be fulfilled in order to qualify for an even higher rate of benefit (and of course there are no contribution conditions at all for the treatment of sickness under the National Health Service); why is unemployment benefit of limited duration whereas sickness benefit may be paid indefinitely; why should the widow of an insured male who has died a natural death be treated quite differently from the widow of a man who has died as a result of an industrial accident; why should the widow who has no private means and so goes out to work in order to supplement her benefit be subjected to a means test on her earnings and may have her benefit reduced, whereas the widow with substantial private means in the form of unearned income is not subject to the 'earnings rule'; why in the case of the expectant mother who has planned to have the baby at home and has probably incurred expenditure in anticipation of the event is the maternity benefit drastically reduced if through no fault of hers she is forced to enter hospital for her confinement and has to stay there for more than seventy-two hours; why is the man who slips on his own doorstep and breaks a leg as he leaves his house in the morning for the express purpose of going to work entitled, if qualified, for sickness benefit whereas had he delayed breaking his leg until he had arrived at his place of employment he may have qualified for a higher industrial injury benefit; why are there substantial differences in the 'social income' provided for the man who has been permanently disabled on active service in war, the man whose disability is due to an accident at home or on the street, and the man who has been 'industrially' disabled; why is it assumed that we all know the separate amounts we pay weekly or monthly into the National Insurance Fund, the Industrial Injuries Fund, and the contribution towards the cost of the National Health Service, and that in some especial and highly significant way we regard them as being quite different from the amount we have to pay in income tax; and why, when statutory deductions are made for most of us by our employers, do we persist in the 'stamp method' of payment for National Insurance contributions and in effect a cash method for income tax?

Attempts have been made to justify differences of these kinds; for example, it has been argued that a more liberal industrial injury benefit is necessary in order to compensate the insured person who works in a dangerous occupation where the chances of an accident are higher than in safe occupations. A reasonable principle, but in practice the nature of the occupation has no bearing on the eligibility of the insured person, and the same rate of benefit is payable to a person injured in an extremely safe occupation as is payable to one in a highly dangerous occupation. We seem to take delight in devising principles which are then nullified in practice, and in developing social policies based on no consistent principles of action. Surely if it is agreed that the state ought to ensure the maintenance of a minimum level of income during periods of interruption or cessation of earnings, then the starting point for a consideration of what kind of system will best achieve that aim ought to be the individual's loss of income, and not the possible factors giving rise to the loss. We now accept, though we did not in the inter-war years, that the same rate of benefit is justifiable whether the need arises out of unemployment or sickness or retirement; why then do we insist on retaining an enormously complex system of categorisation of causes in order to provide for what is basically one need? Presumably because of the intention to apply insurance principles; and these require the calculation on an actuarial basis of the relative risks. Yet from the very first day of the implementation of the National Insurance Act 1946 the actuarial principles were abandoned in respect of retirement pensions.

The Labour Government was fully entitled to take the political decision that retirement pensions at the full rate should be payable immediately instead of (as had been proposed by Lord Beveridge) gradually increasing the rate from an actuarially sound low rate initially to the full rate over a transitional period of twenty years. Having taken this decision, why maintain the façade of insurance for the remaining, and from the point of view of cost and the number of beneficiaries, less vital parts of the scheme? Indeed, in terms of overall cost it is very doubtful whether the abandonment of all contribution conditions would have resulted in any greater financial burden to the community, but it would have led to the elimination of the unnecessary categorisation of 'need' and to a very large reduction in the numbers of administrative 'experts' whose main claim to expertise lies in their knowledge, understanding, and capacity to interpret the complicated contribution conditions which are unintelligible to the average citizen.

The complexity of our systems of income maintenance is in itself a barrier to reasoned discussion so essential for reform. To know and understand the whole system of social security in all its detail is an enormous task, and anyone who claimed to be an expert in the whole field would probably be so weighed down with minutiae as to be almost unable to see the aims, purposes, and methods in relation to the objectives and needs of the community. It is much easier, and of course in line with the traditionalist view of policy-making, to go on as we have been, modifying a little here, adjusting a little there, and accepting that in the main the principles (even if not applied in practice) and the policies which have been applied in the past will continue to operate in the future. Other countries have succeeded in devising schemes far more appropriate for the needs of the second half of the twentieth century, but we seem reluctant even to consider whether the principles designed in 1911 and 1942 are suitable and effective for the quite different social situation of the 1960s. The Labour Party in its 1963 proposals was prepared at long last to abandon some of the so-called principles to which it had held tenaciously, such as flat rates of contribution and benefits, and recognised the case for 'a radical change'. But when the committee which prepared this new policy statement opened its case with this claim: 'Under the Labour Government—when Aneurin Bevan launched the first comprehensive free Health Service in the Western world, and James Griffiths laid the foundations of our modern National Insurance—Britain led the way in social security', one wonders how realistic their proposals were. The Western world in this context is open to a variety of interpretations, but it is to be hoped that the members of the Committee realised that one Commonwealth country, New Zealand, launched a 'free' health service and had a comprehensive system of social security long before 1948, and that some of the Scandinavian countries were by no means backward in the social field at that time. In any case the development of a comprehensive system of social security is too vital an issue to be left in the hands of the political parties, who when out of office (as the Labour Party found in 1957 when they attempted to prepare a plan for 'National Superannuation') cannot have access to the essential data available in government files, and when in office are presumably overburdened with the cares of governing.

When the Labour Party succeeded in becoming the Government in 1964 the new ministers were clearly in a hurry to implement some of the proposals they had made during their long years in opposition, and in 1965 they introduced the Redundancy Payments Act which remedied to some extent at least one of the anomalies of the past. Then in 1966 the Ministry of Social Security Act was passed 'which introduced a number of minor procedural and structural improvements but left untouched the traditional administration of social security. The Ministry of Pensions and National Insurance and the National Assistance Board were abolished as separate departments and were replaced by the Ministry of Social Security which included a semi-autonomous board—the Supplementary Benefits Commission —to do the work of the extinct National Assistance Board'.[3]

These mergers were clearly intended to create a unified system of social security, and further steps were taken to complete this merger in 1968 when the Ministry of Health and the Ministry of Social Security were amalgamated to become the Department of Health and Social Security under the Secretary of State for Social Services.

The trend away from flat rate benefits and contributions was established in 1969 when the Government published a White Paper on *Social Insurance proposals for earnings-related short-term and invalidity benefits*[4] which may well lead to a truly integrated system of full social security. If so, then we will at last have moved towards a basic aim of any welfare state for a truly constructive system of income maintenance.

If our income maintenance policies seem to be directed in a confused way primarily at the right to exist rather than to live the full life, there are a variety of other forms of social action which are expressly intended to provide the opportunity for every one of us to lead as full a life as possible. Of these the most fundamental is concerned with the provision of educational facilities. We tend to forget that 'the right to learn' has only comparatively recently been accorded to the majority of the citizens of Britain, and that in the world as a whole there is still a large proportion of the population which has never been given the opportunity of being taught how to read and write its own language. By comparison with many countries our educational facilities are luxuriant, but are our educational objectives clearly defined and have we rational methods of achieving them?

The prime objective is to ensure that a minimum standard of literacy is attained by all, and in this scientific age there is an increasing emphasis on 'numeracy'. No one (I hope) would deny the right of all to be given the opportunity of becoming literate, and there seems to be no dispute about the best method of achieving this minimal standard, that is through formal teaching in schools. When, as in Britain since 1944, the objectives go beyond the minimum and the right to learn means more than the limited attainment of an ability to read, write, and count, conflicting views emerge about the nature of this further education, its purposes, and the ways in which it should be provided. 'Secondary education for all' may be an acceptable slogan, the right to receive an education appropriate to age, aptitude, and ability may be a sound principle, but what is this additional level of education for, what value is it to the individual and the community, to whom should even higher levels of education be given and on what basis? These are some of the questions which need to be asked and answered by politicians and educationists in a democracy.

In a period of rapid social and economic change, educational objectives may not easily be capable of definition or clarification, and all that is known with certainty is that in recent years we have succeeded in providing secondary education for more young people than ever before in our history. Whether it is the type of education best suited to meet the needs of the second half of the twentieth century and whether all children have equal opportunity to obtain the kind of education most suitable for them are questions which cannot easily be answered. It is, however, certain that the 'grammar school' type of education is by no means equally available throughout the country, and that methods of selection at 11 + are not universally approved. If we believe that different types of education, each having differing values, are essential, then obviously some kind of system of selection is necessary, and as we seem to believe that the traditional grammar school type is the best for the most intelligent pupils the competition for places has become increasingly fierce. Attempts to placate anxious parents by assurances that the secondary modern and the comprehensive are just as good as the grammar school have not proved very effective, and no wonder when the avenues to higher education and to certain kinds of professional training are virtually closed to pupils who have not attended grammar or public schools. In time the gap between the assumed virtues of the traditional grammar and the unproven demerits of 'the modern' may be lessened, and we may find ourselves being more in line with other countries by having a less specialised and less selective system of secondary education, leading presumably to a greater measure of equality of educational opportunity.[5]

Competitive selection is no longer confined to the secondary stage. Entry to the universities and to a lesser extent the teacher training colleges is now highly competitive, and the technical colleges and colleges of advanced technology have increasing numbers of applicants, so that the mad scramble at 18+ has become as notorious as that of the 11+. The change, in a very few years, from an almost non-competitive system of entry to the universities to one where the competition is fantastically intense is a remarkable social phenomenon, and it illustrates vividly the chain reaction process inherent in a progressive social policy. The policy of providing secondary education for all, the emphasis laid on the value of as lengthy a period of education as possible, the increasing demands for specialised education to meet the needs of a technological age, more generous provision by way of grants and scholarships enabling young people to continue their education beyond the normal school leaving age, and many other policies and practices have created the exceptional demands for student places at institutions of higher education. Yet while the forces and pressures favourable to the extension of secondary education were continuously being strengthened, all too little preparation and forethought was being given to the consequential impact on higher education.

One of the reasons for our failure to plan ahead and make adequate preparations for the exceptional demands, foreseeable in the early 1950s and materialising in the early 1960s, for higher education is that the aims of our society in relation to the role and purpose of universities are ambivalent. We cannot make up our minds about the crucial question: university education for whom and for what? Do we want to restrict the number of students at this level of higher education to the chosen few, who will then form the intellectual élite of the community? If so, how should they be chosen and by whom? Or do we want to make it possible for everyone who attains a minimum stipulated standard and desires a university type of education to be given the right of automatic entry?[6] The choice would appear to lie between a highly selective and an open-door system of entry, and the crucial question in a welfare state is which of these alternatives is appropriate? If higher education makes a substantial contribution to the well-being of the community then presumably the greater the number of graduates the greater their contribution; but clearly there are limits to the numbers who can profitably pursue and gain advantage from the numerous specialised courses of study at this level. There are some countries with an open-door system of university entrance where the majority of students choose one field of study which has a limited demand in its practice, with the result that large numbers of unemployable graduates are produced annually. Obviously situations of this kind need to be avoided as they can be if the aims and purposes of higher education are clarified and the separate stages of education are looked upon not as distinct and finite units but as complementary processes in the pursuit of knowledge.

In the modern world 'adequate systems of education at all levels are an essential prerequisite to the economic, social and political development of all countries' (a resolution of the eleventh session of the General Conference of the United Nations Educational Scientific and Cultural Organisation). We in Britain have a relatively long history, compared with many countries, of educational development, and our achievements are the envy of less fortunate peoples, yet while we subscribe to and support the need for planning education as a whole in other countries we allow our own system to develop in piecemeal fashion with no apparent co-ordination of separate policies.

The fragmentation of educational services is perhaps carried to even greater lengths in those fields of education not commonly accepted as part of the schooling system. Ancillary services like child guidance clinics, youth employment advice services, special schools for the physically and mentally handicapped, are all deemed to be essential for the nation, but they are remarkably unevenly provided throughout the country as a whole and vary substantially in their range and quality. And one of the outstanding examples of how national policy, reasonably clearly stated in terms of aims and principles, can be nullified in practice is to be found in the history of the youth service from 1939 to 1969.

In 1939 a Board of Education circular outlined the policy for the creation of a national youth service, but when the Albemarle Committee examined in 1958 and 1959 the youth service in England and Wales its report shows that only a very small part of the policy had in fact been implemented in the previous twenty years.[7] Obviously the war and the claims of other educational services on the national resources in the post-war years meant that priorities had to be determined for overall educational expenditure, but the Committee were, rightly, puzzled by the 'low precedence' accorded by successive Ministers of Education to 'this part of' their 'responsibilities', and were to 'find a picture of somewhat haphazard development' when they examined the contribution of the local authorities to the implementation of national policy. Indeed, even in 1958-9, the Committee found that 'some important authorities have no youth committee and no youth officer. Even authorities that value the service show surprising variations in the way they go about things', and the main argument of the Ministry of Education and the local authorities for failure to develop the service was the lack of finance.

The total direct expenditure on the youth service by the Ministry and all local authorities in 1957-8 was estimated by the Committee to be a little over £2¾ million, equal to one penny per pound of all expenditure on education, a minute sum in relation to our national income in that year. Had we really desired a youth service we could obviously have afforded to spend very much more without endangering national solvency, and the only firm conclusion to be drawn from the dismal picture of a youth service in 'a state of acute depression' is that the decision as to whether the declared policy should be implemented was determined solely on grounds of finance, and not on the basis of the needs of youth and the value of the service in meeting those needs.

Additional expenditure on the youth service in the 1950s may have been accompanied by a reduction in national expenditure on a variety of other services designed for youths such as remand homes, approved schools, and borstals, and the Albemarle Committee argued that an effective youth service leads to an increase in national prosperity by equipping youths 'to live the life of a free society'. But it was not the function of the Ministry of Education to consider balancing factors of that kind, nor indeed was it the responsibility of any other organisation to take an overall view of the impact of one fragment of social policy on social policy as a whole.

Ten years later the situation of the youth service seems to be no better than it was in 1959 despite the fact that the Ministry of Education had become in 1964 the Department of Education and Science and was still responsible for this vital service. Perhaps in a welfare state there is no need for a youth service, but if so then clearly we should make a firm decision.

In other spheres of social action designed to ensure the right to live or to improve living standards the expenditure of public money is all too often thought of in terms only of cost and not of the possibility of returns as well. The fact that spending on one service may lead to considerable savings in expenditure on others, and may even be an investment yielding good national dividends in the future, seems rarely to be considered, and of course the whole financial situation is made immensely more complicated and the possibilities of thwarting the broad aims of social policy are increased by the acceptance of the principle of local implementation.

National policy and local practices are often in conflict over the provision of such diverse services as those for children deprived of a normal home life, the physically and mentally handicapped, the aged, offenders against the law placed on probation, and even that basic necessity of life, housing. The Minister of Housing may set a target of so many thousand houses to be built in a year, the Minister of

Health may decree certain varieties and standards of 'welfare' services, and the Home Secretary may lay down standards of staffing and service in child care and probation, but there can be no assurance of achievement when responsibility for actual performance rests with hundreds of local committees, when no attempt is made to relate the separate aims to each other or to measure the practicability of their attainment.

For years the Minister of Housing has set a target of the number of houses to be built annually, but one wonders how the actual figure is determined when within the Ministry there is no real knowledge of the actual stock of houses already built, their age, conditions, and estimated length of life, nor are systematic attempts made to measure the real future demands for new homes. Ever since their introduction in 1948 the 'welfare services' provided by the local authorities have operated on a hit or miss basis, and the publication of a ten-year plan for 'the health and welfare services, and community care' by the Minister of Health in 1965 showed only too clearly that there was in fact no plan. All that this 'plan' showed was the numbers of staff of various kinds which each local authority thought it would need in the next ten years. We cannot be sure that these figures were no more than a guess, or, even more likely, were just 'thought up' for sending to the Ministry, and in any case no attempt was made by the Ministry to reconcile the very obvious differences in the figures supplied by roughly comparable authorities. Nor was any indication given on the extent to which it was believed that these numbers of specialised personnel would in fact be capable of providing 'health and welfare services' for the nation and on the basis of national standards. Perhaps the Ministry was chary of commenting and of producing a real plan because of the severe criticisms levelled at the statistics used as a basis for its ten-year hospital development plan published in 1962, but, whatever the reason, if the future 'health and welfare' policy is to be based on such inadequate assessments of needs and means as those in these plans, then we are unlikely to see any reduction in the variation of the availability and quality of services from one area to another. And if we continue to plan on the basis of separate services separately controlled and having little or no relation with each other we are unlikely to find a solution to the problem of co-ordination which has bedevilled the field of welfare services for the past sixty years.

The inauguration of the 'new' services in 1948 was confidently expected to result in a smooth merging of functions and co-operation between departments of central and local governments so as to eliminate overlapping and duplication of effort. However, as early as 1950 the Ministries of Education and Health and the Home Office found it necessary to issue a joint circular about the services directed at the needs of neglected and deprived children living in their own homes. Experience had shown that one family was being dealt with by three or four different departments of the same local authority, and possibly two or three other statutory organisations, so the circular recommended that a co-ordinating officer should be appointed in every major local authority to bring together the separate officers by means of a case conference. How effective this system has been is not really known, and of course it makes no contribution to the situation which still exists where a citizen with a relatively simple problem to be solved may find that it requires the separate efforts of an even greater number of civil servants and local government officers, and maybe a variety of workers in voluntary organisations, to provide a solution. The 'new' services have obviously not solved the problems of what would in industrial circles be castigated as demarcation disputes, and it is not surprising that overlapping occurs when, for example, some local authority housing departments have established 'housing welfare services' despite the fact that there is in the same authority a 'welfare department' whose officers could presumably deal just as effectively with housing welfare problems as they do with welfare problems in general.

All these co-ordinating difficulties arise out of the fragmentation of the social services, and the extent to which we perpetuate and accentuate fragmentary policies can be seen in the number and variety of Committees of Inquiry which have officially examined in recent years distinct, and what are presumed to be quite separate, aspects of social policy. For example, one Committee has examined the field of work of health visitors; another investigated the employment of social workers in the health and welfare services of local authorities; another looked at the management of local authority housing, which in effect meant assessing the work of housing managers, some of whom claim to be primarily concerned with welfare; yet another looked at the functions and conditions of service of probation officers, and another the 'welfare work' involved in dealing with the after-care of prisoners. Most of these committees must have found that by confining themselves to the specified category of worker or service detailed in their terms of reference they were creating artificial boundaries inimical to a proper understanding of the role of their subject, and that they had to neglect the fundamental issue of relationship with allied workers and services. The real tragedy is that not once in the past fifteen years has any committee examined the whole field of social welfare or the inter-relatedness of the artificially created separate pieces of social policy. As long as we persist in categorising needs, and implying that 'welfare' is limited to the aid given to certain specified groups, and while our social aims are as confused and conflicting as they are now, so long will the tangled maze of separatist policies remain, and principles, policies, and practices conflict with each other.

Even the long awaited Seebohm Report[8] was in effect restricted by its terms of reference, but if it is implemented then we may at least see some degree of integration of social service departments within local authorities, which is surely a step in the right direction.

The basic aim of the right to protection and community support when one is incapacitated physically or mentally is of course pursued in this country by an array of services provided under Public Health legislation, the National Health Service, and voluntary organisations.[9] The aims seem clear but again we indulge in our favourite pastime of fragmentary implementation which will perhaps become less fragmented if the proposals in the Green Paper published by the Ministry of Health in 1968 are implemented.[10]

It cannot be claimed that as yet we have perfect health services, but certainly we have a range of services as good, and in many cases better, than those of many other countries, and perhaps above all else there is no longer the fear of being unable to obtain treatment and care in this country as there was in the past and as there still is in some countries even more affluent than ours.

There are still needs and problems requiring urgent attention in our welfare state which are only partially met. For example, the needs and problems of the aged, which, although they have been the subject of numerous investigations beginning effectively with *Old people— a Report of a Survey Committee on the Problems of Ageing and the Care of Old People* published by the Nuffield Foundation in 1947, and numerous reports thereafter,[11] have by no means been solved. There is too a growing recognition that the physically handicapped are not as well provided for as they should be, and that there are still many homeless persons as well as many living in substandard houses and so on. In short the aims and achievements of the welfare state are by no means complete.

What we now require is a rational objective assessment of the main aims of social policy in relation to the kind of society we want ours to be, and of the methods of achieving them. If we genuinely believe that the aims of a welfare state must include at least the right of every child born to be given an equal chance to live, to be educated, and to develop skills commensurate with his or her ability, and in adulthood to the right to work, to a minimum standard of life, and to contribute to the well-being of the community, then we must decide how these aims can best be attained. Should they be determined by 'market forces' so that, for example, the chances of living from birth and the kinds of education received will depend on the individual capacity of parents to buy medical, educational, and other services, or should we rely on social provision? Questions of this kind have not as yet been clarified in our society, and they never will be as long as we persist in acting on unproven assumptions, ill-defined standards and values, and half-truths and myths about the nature, purpose, and functions of the state and its citizens.

Declared aims can, in a complex society, be achieved only by designed means, and both are the result of the thought processes of human beings. Who makes, controls, and directs policies in the welfare state is a question rarely asked, and even more rarely examined. If it were, then one fact at least would be revealed, and that is that the haphazard, ill-defined, and unco-ordinated policies and practices, seen by many people as constituting an essential feature of the welfare state, have been made by men, and have given rise to enormous administrative units controlled by politicians and administrators, whose powers over the lives and destinies of the rest of us are far greater than is commonly assumed.

# The decision-making and administrative problems of maintaining a welfare state

4

One of the outstanding features of the political and economic history of Britain in the twentieth century is the phenomenal growth in the power and influence of the state, and hence in the changed relationship between the citizen and his elected government. Even at the end of the nineteenth century the average citizen, unless he committed an offence at law, had very little contact with governmental officials of any kind, but by the middle of the twentieth century the chances are remote for even the most law-abiding citizen to go through life without coming into contact, either directly or indirectly, with a variety of officials of central and local government and other public authorities. The citizen is made to realize only too clearly, and with monotonous regularity, the degree of contact he has to maintain with officialdom; but to what extent has the selection and training of officials been changed; how have public servants adjusted themselves to the more frequent personal contacts they have to make with citizens; what limits have been set to the power of officials; and how has the machinery of administration been modified so as to take account of the changed situation? Questions like these until relatively recently were rarely raised in public discussions, and in the main we seem to have allowed the machinery of government and those who operated it to remain undisturbed as if no changes had occured in the relationship between the citizen and the state, and in its powers over the lives and well-being of its citizens.

Is it a *sine qua non* of a welfare state that administrative tribunals, power-conscious central and local government departments, and autocratic officials must flourish? Or is it that in our haphazard methods of development we neglected to consider the possibility of new methods of administration to meet the needs of a changing society, and so have become saddled with traditional administrative systems designed to serve the limited range of governmental functions in the nineteenth century? Undoubtedly we have relied too much on the traditional methods of administration whose salient features were a machine-like inexorability, anonymity, exclusiveness, and separation from the rest of society. The administrators were assumed to be political eunuchs whose functions were to execute policy made by their political masters, and their methods of work were clearly defined by regulations, rigidly limited in a hierarchical system of responsibility and power allowing for no independence of thought. Under these conditions departments of state were primarily concerned with maintaining the *status quo*, and by very selective recruitment of staff, narrow in-service training, strict adherence to the rules and to precedents, and by establishing a tradition of impartiality in political affairs, they became powerful instruments resistant to change. The result was that, while the functions of government were continually expanding and changing, the machinery of government hardly changed at all in its methods of procedure, organisation, or routine.

The necessity of creating new departments of state in the first half of the twentieth century gave an opportunity for innovations to be made in the forms of organisation and the methods of running them, but the new Ministries of Labour, Health, Housing and Local Government, and Pensions and National Insurance were all designed as replicas of those already well established, in some cases for centuries, whose forms of procedure changed but little despite radical alterations in their functions. The Treasury is the prime example of the well-established traditional department attempting to deal with mid-twentieth-century problems of government with a form of organisation and procedures well suited to eighteenth- or at best nineteenth-century conditions. Only very recently were economists and statisticians recruited to its staff, and it is only since 1963 that this organisation, with its wide-ranging powers over the whole civil service, its control of state expenditure, and thus indirectly the economic effort of the nation, had at its head a triumvirate of three 'top' officials, one of whom became responsible for the affairs of the

Cabinet, another the financial and economic work of the government and the third the management of the civil service. Between 1953 and 1963 these vast and distinct functions were in the hands of two men, and before 1956 it was apparently considered practicable for one man to carry these responsibilities. The announcement, in July 1962, of the three projected appointments was hailed as a sign that henceforth the Treasury is to be organised along functional lines, and that administrators and economic experts are to be more closely integrated. Whether this new form of management will lead to greater efficiency, a more imaginative approach to economic and social problems, less of the stop-go financial policies of recent years, and the gradual elimination of what has been so often in the past 'the dead hand of the Treasury' cannot now be assessed because from 1964 onwards radical changes appear to have been made in the number and types of government departments.

New departments have been established, such as the Department of Economic Affairs; some have had their responsibilities widened, such as the former Ministry of Education which in 1964 became the Department of Education and Science; others have been merged, such as the Ministry of Social Security and the Ministry of Health which in 1968 became the Department of Health and Social Security, while the Ministry of Defence has presumably taken over the functions of the Admiralty, the War Office and the Air Ministry; and others have acquired new titles, such as the Ministry of Labour which has become the Department of Employment and Productivity. How far these new titles have resulted in a radical change of functions and responsibilities remains to be seen, but the new titles may be indicative of a new approach towards the fulfilment of social policies. There is, however, some uncertainty as to the relationship of the Treasury to the Department of Economic Affairs though it seems that the Treasury (despite having lost its function of recruitment and training of civil servants which is now, as a result of the recommendations of the Fulton Committee,[1] the responsibility of a new Civil Service Department) is still paramount in financial matters.

The ways in which the Treasury performs its duties, the basis for its calculations of size and quality of staff in other government departments, the limits on expenditure for all government services, the incentives for, or restraints on, economic activity in general, and the myriad other responsibilities it has to fulfil, are shrouded in mystery. But what is certain is that day in and day out decisions affecting the economic well-being of the nation and the welfare of all citizens are taken at Treasury level, and that annually the estimates of expenditure by all other departments are scrutinized and authorised by this crucial, pivotal organisation, In effect, the nation's social and economic policies are to a considerable degree under Treasury control. How, one wonders, does it reconcile the competing claims of projected expenditure on, for example, education as against health services, or housing, or child care, or old people's welfare, or export credits, or the armed services, or foreign aid, or state banquets, or the prevention of crime, or ministerial jaunts abroad, or Royal Commissions, and the thousands of other claims on the government purse? Presumably by careful consideration of the case put forward by the claimants, and by reference to the overall demands in relation to the total possible expenditure, which will, of course, be influenced by the inclinations, aspirations, and prognostications of the political masters of the Treasury.

Ultimate decisions on state expenditure must obviously be taken by the politicians in office, and it is with them that responsibility lies for saying 'Yes' or 'No'. Yet it is difficult to believe that a newly appointed Chancellor of the Exchequer (and there have been a number in recent years) can master in a matter of hours the intricate and complex details of state expenditure so as to arrive completely independently at a decision. Surely the fact is that the pros and cons of a suggested course of action are presented to the Chancellor (or any other minister), and from the alternatives presented he makes his choice. Who, then, is the real decision-maker: is it the politician or the administrator?

Administrators in central and local government vehemently deny that they make decisions, and the doctrine of ministerial responsibility strengthens the claim that it is the politician who takes and accepts responsibility for a decision. But taking and accepting responsibility is not necessarily synonymous with making a decision, and it is in the making that the administrative machine comes into its own. Systematic case studies of decision-making in all fields of human activity are all too rare. Not very much is known about the way in which major decisions in industry and commerce are made even though they may affect the livelihood of millions of people, and when attempts are made by independent research workers to study the processes and pressures involved in arriving at a business decision they are often thwarted by the power, and presumably the right, of business men to refuse access to essential data. However, the results of various courses of action taken by industrial and commercial organisations can be seen and examined and measured in the form of profit and loss, the creation of employment or unemployment, and in the production of goods and services; and at least we know where power lies and the motives for particular forms of action. The main aim of any business man is to make a profit, and the organisation he creates is designed to achieve that end. Business administration, therefore, is a means to a declared end, and if the end is not achieved then the organisation is usually dissolved. But in the field of government the ends are not always clear and the results are not easily measurable, so that there is no simple test of the effectiveness of the administrative organisations. Furthermore, with the security of tenure granted to public servants, and the assumed permanence of government departments, the administrative machine tends to be self-perpetuating, immune to tests of efficiency, and builds within itself powerful pressure groups resistant to change or elimination.

The basic structure of administrative units in the public services varies little, irrespective of their functions. Whether they deal with people or with things has little bearing on the methods of organisation, the forms of procedure, and the system of communications within and with persons and groups outside the organisation. The similarities between the multifarious central government departments makes it possible for the British theory to be propounded that, even in these days of specialisation, an administrator is capable of running equally well any department. Having spent many years in, say, the Ministry of Agriculture and Fisheries an administrative class male (or more rarely female) can then quite possibly move to Housing or Education or the Home Office, or any other department.

The advantages of moving administrators from one kind of department to another are, theoretically, considerable, but there are equally obvious disadvantages as the functions of each department become more highly specialised and disparate. The main functions of a government department are to provide information and advice to assist the minister in the making of policy and then to carry out that policy, and surely, therefore, civil servants must of necessity become specialists in the field of work of the ministry. But again there is the British tradition that the head of a department is first and last an administrator and need not be expert in the technical functions of the ministry: a tradition still fervently maintained and enshrined in a cardinal principle of civil service administration, that administrators must always be on top and have, around but beneath them, experts on tap. This tradition is, perhaps, slowly being lost because in recent years the recruitment of a variety of experts has been greatly accelerated and in-service training within the service is being modernised.

The training of public servants is, of course, of vital importance,[2] but to enable them to reach the right decisions on matters of policy they need facts which often can only be acquired by systematic research.

The need for research into the factors giving rise to social problems, or even for the accumulation of basic data, was hardly recognised by government departments in the past. For example, for many years the state accepted the responsibility for dealing with and attempting to prevent crime, and the Home Office for the past eighty odd years has produced annually statistics purporting to show the incidence of crime; yet it was not until 1950 that a statistician was appointed, and a research unit established. Since the end of the Second World War the state has played a vital part in the provision of housing, yet the amount of research carried out by the Ministry of Housing into housing needs was pathetically small; from 1948 the state accepted full responsibility for the National Health Service, yet a new Minister of Health complained bitterly in 1962 of the inadequacy of hospital statistics. And in October 1962 a new Minister of Education, in an interview reported in *New Society* (No. 2, 11 October 1962), was clearly determined to see that the statistical services of the Ministry were maintained at all costs, and went on to state that in the first ten years after the war 'the country tried to have more purposive government with very inadequate statistics', which is a polite way of saying that most of our social policies were designed and implemented without adequate knowledge. Not many ministers have been as forthright as the Minister of Health was in 1962, and not many have declared publicly, as the Minister of Education did in 1962, their belief in the need for facts on which to base policy and for making 'the most use possible of solid rational enquiry'.

Encouraging as it was to hear ministers complain about the inadequacy of research facilities they must surely bear at least part of the blame for not demanding adequate data, and, indeed, for not making more use of an admirable research unit set up by the Coalition Government during the war, the Social Survey Unit of the Central Office of Information. This Unit has since become the Government Social Survey Department and carries out research for any department of state. It has, over the years, done excellent work, but clearly it was not capable of doing all the research needed to provide all the information required for the development of social policy.

Since 1965 research units or sections have been established in most departments and there seems now to be a genuine interest in prosecuting research. Some departments not only carry out research within the department but also finance research projects by outside organisations like universities. In addition, of course, there is by now a national Social Science Research Council which finances social research on a scale very different from that of the past.[3] It looks as though the interest in social research of all kinds is now greater than it has ever been before, indeed we may well be indulging in research on a scale unthinkable in the past and perhaps over-luxurious now. However, the change in attitude towards obtaining relevant information in the years 1965–1969 can only be described as remarkable but we shall, of course, have to wait some time before assessing how effective this change has been.

In some ways, we have relied in the past, and still do, not so much on research but on the advice of advisory committees to provide guide lines for the development of social policy. There are now in Britain hundreds of advisory committees of various kinds. Some are created by Act of Parliament, serve as a permanent advice body in relation to policy-making, and are therefore an essential part of the machinery of democratic government; others may be appointed ad hoc by ministers to give their views on specific problems, and there are advisory committees which in effect are used to reflect public opinion. The purposes for which they are used, the extent to which their advice is sought and acted upon, vary widely, but even if the civil service were composed entirely of experts many committees would still be necessary, and indeed essential, in a democracy. However, they ought not to be used, as they sometimes have been, as a face-saving device for a government which cannot or will not make up its mind, nor as a façade, as they sometimes are, giving to the outside world the appearance that a minister and his department are earnestly and sincerely seeking the views of a representative body of opinion on vital issues of policy, when in fact by restrictive terms of reference and determination of the agenda for meetings the contribution which members can make is deliberately limited; and of course they ought never to be used as an excuse whereby departments avoid doing the work that their servants are paid to do. Obviously advisory bodies and committees of inquiry have their uses and their limitations, and a crucial factor in determining their value is the quality of the members.

The membership of official committees, who is appointed by whom and for what reasons, is a subject in itself worthy of investigation. Some of the appointments, of course, are self-evident—for example, when an expert committee is formed to study a highly technical and specialised problem—but so often the membership has to be spread over representative interests—for example, of employers, employees, local authorities, other interested organisations, and supporters of the political parties; and often one wonders why is it that Mr X was chosen and not Mr Y, and, on occasion, was Mr X really suitable? Who decides the membership, and on what basis? Is it the minister or the administrators? It cannot surely be the minister alone, even though he is ultimately responsible for issuing the invitation; and presumably therefore persons are appointed as a result of suggestions made by politicians, administrators, and various kinds of pressure groups. Critics of this method argue that it is undemocratic, but is it necessarily more dangerous than choosing the members through a system of elections? There is obviously the danger of political party bias, but in practice there seems to be a deliberate attempt made to ensure that if a person or persons known to be of one party is or are appointed then the other side is represented as well, and there are, of course, many committees where the political faiths of the members are irrelevant. Imperfect as the methods of selection may be, the fact is that some committees in recent years have produced stimulating reports objectively critical of the department which appointed them and even of government policy. However, the question still remains to be answered of how far committees of outsiders should be expected to do the thinking for government departments and politicians.

If the function of a ministry is simply to provide the machinery for implementing policy made by politicians then all that can be expected of administrators is that they ensure that the machine works. Thinking about policy must be the responsibility of the politician, and in these circumstances every change of party in power could mean a reversal of state policies. In fact, of course, this does not happen, in part, perhaps, because the differences on major policy issues between the main political parties are not as marked as they would like us to believe, and even more fundamentally because of the extreme reliance of politicians in power on the permanent officials. It has been said, and not without good reason, that a minister is utterly dependent on the relationships he forms and the support he succeeds in obtaining from the officials, and this is inevitable in a system where the official post, once established, goes on for ever whereas a minister is but a temporary incumbent of his office. Why not, therefore, recognise the logical consequences of this relationship by acknowledging that officials must contribute substantially to the making of policy, and that the kind of officials appointed will determine the types of policy adopted as much as, if not more than, the elected politicians?

The British people have an inherent distrust of 'officialdom', and officials seek to make it abundantly clear that they have no power and no wish to acquire it. But with the increasing complexity of economic, social, and political activities, and the ever-expanding range of influence and control over individual actions by the state, official powers have had to be given to the holders of official offices, and whether they like it or not they exercise and must have power. The park attendant who orders us to keep off the grass in accordance with a by-law has power; the hundreds of officials who are entitled to enter our homes without a search warrant have power; the officer of the Supplementary Benefits Commission or the Department of Health and Social Security who decides entitlement to benefit or assistance has power; the chief education officer who directs that a child may go to one school but not another has power; the head of a university department who decides which of the hundreds of applicants he will admit as students to his department has power; the planning officer who decides that a wooden shed cannot be built in the back garden of No. 1 Acacia Avenue has power; and there are thousands of officials who in pursuance of their duties have to exercise power whether they like it or not. But this does not mean that ours is a police state in which power is given to officials deliberately to curtail individual freedom. In nearly all cases the powers are strictly limited and most important of all when they are exercised they can usually be appealed against.

The increase in the number of officials exercising power has been accompanied by an elaborate system of appeals through courts of law, and in more recent years through a variety of specially created tribunals.[4] Members of the courts and the tribunals in turn exercise power, sometimes final and sometimes subject to higher authority; but at some stage a final decision has to be made by someone. And this is a fact that all too often seems to be ignored: that decisions are made by people and not by machines or systems. It may be that a decision can only be made in a certain way because of rules and regulations, but they too have been made by people—all too often, however, under a cloak of anonymity and in conditions of secrecy which create the impression that policy-making and its implementation are processes in which human beings play no part.[5]

Administration, even in these days of electronic computers, is a human process, yet we persist in regarding it simply as a system; and by rigidly defining functions on a hierarchical and authoritarian basis we restrict freedom of thought on the part of each member of the administrative chain so that all he or she has to do is virtually to act mechanically. The use of the terms 'class', and, within each 'class', 'grades', to describe the status and functions of every civil servant is itself significant, and the rigid demarcation of 'divisions', 'branches', and 'sections' within departments creates barriers against the movement of thoughts and ideas vertically and horizontally within the organisation.[6] Obviously divisions of responsibility, and of executive and advisory powers, are inevitable in any large-scale organisation, but the divisions should be designed to promote and not impede thought and action. If a commercial organisation suffers a holdup in one of its divisions it must find a remedy or risk substantial loss. But within a ministry or local authority there can be holdups for years while one person retains a letter in his or her pending tray and the rest of the organisation carries on blissfully unaware of the blockage.

The situation becomes ludicrous when one division within a ministry is unaware of what another is doing, and farcical when, within a division one section has no knowledge that another is dealing with a given problem. Yet these situations are not uncommon and lead to the position where more than one civil servant is usually necessary before the answer to a simple question can be given. 'Passed to you please for comment', 'I shall have to discuss this with my colleagues', 'I shall have to look up the files', and all the other euphemisms commonly used to indicate the variety of persons through whose hands one piece of paper has to be passed before a decision is taken are no longer words; they constitute established practice, limiting initiative of thought and action. Yet oddly enough if a question is asked in Parliament—the dreaded P.Q.—the answer (not necessarily the right one) can usually be found quite quickly. There would seem therefore to be at least two channels of communication, the one tortuous and lengthy used to deal with questions from ordinary citizens and the other speedy and direct which is used when Parliament is in session.

Many examples could be given of where administration appears to be a mechanical process rather than a human activity of thought and action, but more important are the consequences for the development and implementation of social policy. If administrators have become so restricted in outlook, so accustomed to the strait-jacket of rules of procedure, of hierarchical status, of departmentalism, and of rigidly limited functions, how can policy be dynamic? It cannot, if top-level administrators are so involved in ensuring the smooth running of a machine, and so overburdened with trivial details which have to be syphoned through the wide-based bottle, where there is no responsibility at the base, into the narrow spout containing all responsibility, that there is no time for them to sit aside and think about the present aims and practices, and what ought to be the future policies of the department. What time can senior officials have for assessing changing needs, for testing the effectiveness of the policies they have helped to make and are responsible for implementing, when they are immersed in the daily round of being at the beck and call of ministers, required constantly to make decisions, often away for days on end at international meetings, expected to address national conferences, and to keep up to date with the ever-growing body of knowledge applicable to their job? Obviously very little, and being human they will naturally be more concerned with maintaining the status quo rather than creating even more problems for themselves by having bright ideas which, if adopted, might result in turmoil within the organisation. The smallest addition to existing functions may swell disproportionately the responsibilities of senior administrators, and though the dangers of Parkinson's Law must always be borne in mind, it must be recognised that adding functions may cause the organisation to become even more sluggish and reduce the time for constructive thought on the part of those who run it.

Administrators themselves are in an ambivalent position when faced with the offer of additional functions for their department. On the one hand new and additional functions bring added status and power, on the other additional responsibilities, and in a status-ridden society the chances of acquiring greater status may outweigh the burdens of added responsibilities. The choice would be less difficult if the responsibility for making decisions were not channelled into so few hands, and the time may well have arrived when the traditional patterns of departments and the established levels of responsibility may have to be revised. If, for example, instead of (as in most cases in the civil service) one permanent secretary there were a triumvirate of equal 'heads', then one of the three might spend all his or her time thinking about policy.

Since 1965 some departments seem to be moving into a position where the number of top level staff is greater than in the past and with the reallocation and reorganisation suggested by the Fulton Committee there may yet be considerable structural changes in the future. One change in the relationship of the official to the citizen has already occurred which has to some extent humanised this relationship.

Traditionally the accepted means of contact between a ministry and the public was by letter, and until 1948, when Sir Ernest Gowers at the invitation of the Treasury produced his *Plain Words*, there was a form of official English which was almost incomprehensible even to intelligent citizens. Since the publication of that brilliant analysis of 'officialese' and the suggestions made 'to help officials in their use of written English' there has been a marked improvement in the style and tone of official letters and documents. However, problems of communication still remain where 'legal' English has of necessity to be used in the wording of Acts of Parliament and statutory rules and regulations, and with the enormous increase in recent years of the quantity of 'law' relating to the rights and duties of ordinary citizens, which we are presumed to know, the difficulties are greater than ever. Some ministries have attempted to minimise the difficulties by interpreting the law for the citizen in simple English through the medium of pamphlets and leaflets. The Ministry of Pensions and National Insurance was particularly active in producing information leaflets and pamphlet 'guides' to the National Insurance Acts and Regulations; but invariably the warning is given that 'this leaflet gives general guidance on the subject. It must not be treated as a complete and authoritative statement of the law on any particular case'. So that even conscientious reading of the leaflets is no safeguard, and in the main 'guides' the reader is usually advised that 'if you have a problem about national insurance, the staff at your local office will be glad to help you'. Face-to-face contact is therefore presumed to be an essential means of communication, but what evidence is there that in the training given to civil servants emphasis is now laid on the arts of oral as distinct from written communication, and on the art (or is it a science?) of human relations?

There is tangible evidence of an attempt by the National Assistance Board and continued by the Supplementary Benefits Commission to make its officers aware of the nature of human and social problems, and of the principles involved in establishing good relationships between people. Officers are encouraged and given facilities to attend specially designed courses at, for example, the extra-mural departments of some universities, where through systematic study attempts are made to help them understand the complex and delicate task of dealing with 'persons in need'. It is difficult to assess the extent to which this enlightened approach by the Board and its officers has been successful in making the services provided truly personal, but from the comments made by some of the recipients of National Assistance and discussions with some of the officers of every grade it seems clear that there is a very different attitude on the part of most officers to the way in which their job should be performed from that of the Poor Law officers of the not so distant past. Eradicating the reputation for callousness which its predecessor, the Poor Law, had earned for itself was a herculean task for the National Assistance Board, and it may well be that had the Board set out to fulfil its functions by placing more emphasis on administrative procedures and less on personal relations then the stigma of having to depend on 'relief' would still be as marked as it was in the past.

The importance attached to understanding the problems of human relations seemed not to be as evident in the administration of National

Insurance as it was in National Assistance, yet both organisations dealt with basically the same problem—the maintenance of income. If a citizen had to apply for National Insurance benefit the process was essentially impersonal. Form N.I. So and So had to be filled in, and not all the details required on all the forms are intelligible to ordinary mortals; then the applicant had to wait for the mysterious processes of reception, verification, and certification to be completed in some unknown office before the result was known. For example, an honest, conscientious, hard-working, and worthy citizen is injured on his way home from work, and because of the seriousness of his injuries he is taken to hospital: when the harassed wife recovers from the shock and realises that she will now have to make application for a sickness benefit under the National Insurance scheme she will be faced with form-filling requiring efforts of memory, knowledge of her husband's affairs, and a capacity to answer formal questions which would be beyond the powers of most people even if no shock had occurred. If she succeeds in completing the formalities she may still have to wait seven days or more before benefit is paid and thereafter contact will usually be maintained by letter. If the husband has to stay in hospital for many months, when he is discharged she will doubtless be informed immediately that as the insured person has now returned home sickness benefit is no longer payable, and this despite the fact that he has been sent home to recuperate and may not be able to resume work for many months more.

This illustration is not a figment of the imagination; it actually happened, and during many months while the husband was in hospital contact between the Ministry and the insured person's wife was maintained by letters, form-filling, and occasional phone calls made by the wife to clear up ambiguities. The National Assistance Board, whose officers were concerned with the same case, adopted a totally different approach in that contact was maintained by personal visits to the home and occasional requests for information. Why this substantial difference in the methods of establishing relationships and in the procedures?

One reason of course is that officials concerned with contributory benefits have to work strictly within the framework of rules and regulations and have no discretionary powers. One wonders, however, whether all the rules and regulations are strictly necessary and whether in fact it would be more costly to abandon many of them and allow more discretion on the part of officials. It may well be that as a result of the creation of an integrated Department of Health and Social Security and the movement of public servants from contributory to the non-contributory sides that a greater awareness of the need for human relationships will develop. We shall have to wait and see, though it is important to remember that the necessity of staffing government departments concerned with providing personal services to individual human beings by officers having exceptional personal qualities was clearly recognised in the first decade of the twentieth century when plans were made to establish labour exchanges. The main architects of the plan for setting up a national system of labour (or, as they are now called, employment) exchanges were Mr William Beveridge and Mr Herbert Llewellyn Smith, and they urged most strongly that the managers of the new offices should be selected and appointed primarily for their knowledge of the problems the exchanges were intended to solve, and for their personal qualities for dealing with people: qualities not necessarily to be found in the traditional civil servant, and not necessarily capable of being acquired through the usual methods of training within the civil service. The result was that a special scheme of recruitment and selection was devised, and the first managers were therefore appointed on a rational basis. This revolutionary idea—that an administrator needed not only intellectual ability but also particular qualities of personality—appears by now to have become accepted as a principle of selection of civil servants, and the Civil Service Commissioners insist not only on a high level of educational attainment but on personal qualities as well for entry into the administrative grade. But there would appear to be no direct relationship between the personal qualities found in the candidate and the department in which he is, if successful, placed, nor is there any certainty that an applicant with particular personal qualities who is first posted to an appropriate department will necessarily remain in it. Again changes may result in future as a result of the Fulton Report.

If the division of functions, powers, and responsibilities of individuals within government departments needs to be reconsidered in view of changed economic and social conditions and relationships between the state and its citizens, so too is there a real need to review and revise the functions, powers, and responsibilities of the departments in relation to other organisations, especially local authorities and other statutory bodies. The powers of central over local government departments vary widely, and range from being allowed tentatively and with great reluctance to drop a hint as to a possible course of action to a complete and absolute power of enforcement. Often the relative powers are not firmly defined, and not always made clear, but what is obvious is the reluctance of locally elected authorities ever to believe that Whitehall may be right, and the terror in the hearts of those in Whitehall that they may give the impression of appearing to be dictating a course of action to local bodies.

In a democracy the relationships between central and local authorities cannot and ought not to be rigidly defined and inflexible. The use of compulsion, persuasion, and advice in varying degrees would seem to be most acceptable, but there ought surely to be consistent principles underlying the choice of mandatory or permissive powers. Why, for example, is a housing authority compelled to adopt certain standards of house building and is made to conform to planning rules, whereas it is not forced to adopt a rational or equitable rent policy or humane tenancy conditions; why does the Home Secretary have to approve the appointment of a chief constable and a principal (and even senior) probation officer whereas ministerial approval is not required for the appointment of town clerks, municipal treasurers, medical officers of health, chief education officers, and children's officers; why does the Minister of Transport have to approve the siting of a pedestrian crossing but not street lights? Inconsistencies may be valuable in the diverse network of relationships between the central and other statutory authorities, but a muddled division of responsibilities and a tortuous system of decision-making, with a reluctance to accept that ultimate responsibility on many (if not most) of the activities of local authorities in fact now lies with the central government, are hardly conducive to administrative efficiency.

The myth that local government is completely independent of central government control dies hard, despite the fact that even in those spheres of activity where there is no power of compulsion the central government can, and does, ultimately determine what may be done locally by its control of finance. If a local authority wishes to embark on a project in which the central government appears to have no direct interest, for example the building of a swimming bath, then usually approval is required for raising a loan to finance the project, and there are many areas in the country without a swimming bath simply because of failure to obtain 'loan sanction'. The control of the purse by the central authority is now extraordinarily extensive, and therefore the degree of independence of action allowed to local authorities is negligible.

Where the central government is directly involved in the activities of local authorities, as, for example, in the provision of education, health, housing, police, fire, child care, and welfare services, the degree of independence allowed to each authority is relatively small. Not only is finance strictly controlled, but standards of performance are laid down and have to be fulfilled, and it is the recommending or enforcing of standards that often creates confusion. The usual method of ensuring standards of service is by inspection, and in government departments there is by now an imposing array of inspectorates with a variety of kinds of experts and varying degrees of power.

The effectiveness of a human inspectorial system cannot easily be measured, in part because inspectors, being human themselves, have to rely essentially on subjective judgements and have few (if any) mechanical aids with which to test the performance of other human beings in particular fields of work. They may of course devise indices of performance and achievement as guides to their evaluation, but in the main the conclusions arrived at after an inspection of the way in which, for example, a school teacher, policeman, child-care and probation officer does his job will be based on subjective judgements. This is not to say that more objective and even scientific methods of measurement can never be devised, and indeed there is an urgent and pressing need for more research into possible methods of measurement of efficiency and of achievements in these fields of service. At present, however, we assume (and not entirely without justification) that the standards of services of these kinds have been raised by the use of inspectorates. But who determines the range of functions powers, and responsibilities of inspectors, and what is their relationship to administrators and to the persons inspected?

In some ministries there is a clearly defined division between inspectorial and administrative functions; in others the inspectorate becomes embroiled in and dominated by the administrative machine. Where the latter prevails then all too often the inspectors tend to be so administratively minded that the fulfilment of their real functions is impeded by over-emphasising the necessity for conforming to administrative procedures, a reluctance to make or take quick decisions, and on occasion a refusal to give a decision of any kind until their views have been duly and laboriously passed through all the usual channels. One wonders how competent administrators are to examine the views of specialists and on what grounds they reach a conclusion; and there is, of course, the added danger of constructive proposals made after an inspection simply being left on the files with no action taken because administrators are incapable of appreciating the value of the expert suggestions. A system of inspection is not (and ought not to be) just a matter of ensuring that a service is looked at; it should be an aid to the making and re-shaping of policy and practice, an essential means of gathering information on what is being done so as to enable decisions to be made as to what ought and should be done.

If there is some doubt about the action taken on inspectors' reports within a department, there is evidence of the reluctance of some ministries to reveal all the contents of an inspector's report to those who have been inspected. For example, the Probation Division of the Home Office after one (or more) of its inspectors has carried out a full-scale inspection of the probation service in a local area does not make available to the local probation committee a copy of the inspector's report to the Home Secretary; but the inspector *is* allowed to discuss his conclusions orally with the committee. The

Morison Committee considered a proposal that copies of the inspectors' written reports should be sent to probation committees[7] but by some curious and far from logical reasoning rejected the proposal, and supported the existing practice. Surely the inspectors' assessment of the service provided locally is of considerable importance to a probation committee whose duty it is to ensure the efficiency of the service in its area? It is, of course, essential for the Home Secretary to know that adequate services are, or are not, being provided in each area, but it is more than essential for the members of each probation committee to know whether its officers are providing an efficient service: it is absolutely vital. Yet the situation could arise under the existing procedure where the Home Secretary could be better informed than the members of the local committee.

The Morison Committee did not suggest that there should be no communication with the inspected, but are there not dangers in partial information to one party and full to the other? There is at the very least a suspicion that the central authority is not wholly prepared to enter into a full and frank relationship with local probation committees, and inevitably this leads to a feeling of disquiet, even mistrust, of the motives and methods of the people in Whitehall. Such suspicions may be quite unjustifiable. Nevertheless it is difficult for members of local probation committees, who are giving voluntary public service, to avoid the impression that the administrators at the Home Office are unnecessarily holding on to power for its own sake, and this impression is strengthened when the practices of other ministries, especially the Ministry of Education, are compared. The inspectorial functions of the Ministry of Education in relation to the education services provided by local authorities are broadly similar to those of the Home Office in relation to local probation services, but how different are their methods! After an inspection of the local services Her Majesty's Inspectors of Education make available to the local authority a copy of the written report sent to the Minister, which of course leads to a relationship of confidence between the Ministry and the local education authorities of inestimable value in the development of educational policies. Why is it that the Ministry of Education adopts this sensible and rational procedure?

Is it because the inspectorial and administrative functions are clearly distinguished in the Ministry of Education?

Secrecy is, in certain circumstances, essential and justifiable in the collection and retention of information by state officials, but it can be carried to excess, and it may well be that with the radical extension of the functions of the state into purely national affairs the concept of secrecy imposed by the Official Secrets Acts of 1911 and 1920 on all civil servants is too rigidly interpreted. The quantity of information vital to the security of the state in ministries concerned primarily with national welfare services is probably exceedingly small, yet the civil servants employed in them are bound to an oath designed essentially for defence and foreign affairs. Obviously it would not be practicable to exempt some civil servants from obedience to rules designed for all, and in practice ministries have paid particular attention in recent years to the classification of documents so that in all probability the number and variety of secret papers in home affairs departments are very small. Nevertheless, even though most civil servants may not in fact be concerned with secret information during most of their working lives, the effect of the Official Secrets Acts, with their solemn warnings about not divulging information of any kind, is to make civil servants extremely cautious of discussing anything connected with their official duties. This extreme caution may even be extended to official publications, where the cloak of official secrecy may be used as an excuse for avoiding publication of information which ought to be made available in the public interest, and it may well have been responsible for government departments in the past denying genuine research workers access to official sources of data.

Within government departments, central and local, there are vast amounts of data of many kinds of inestimable value to research workers and unobtainable from any other source. In the course of their ordinary duties civil servants and local government officers with the power conferred on them by statutory authority have to collect information which no independent person could possibly obtain. Much of this information is collected for administrative purposes only, but to the research worker it constitutes essential data for adding to knowledge in many fields of inquiry, especially those concerned with unravelling social problems and contributing to knowledge of social conditions. Yet many research workers in universities and other institutions concerned with the prosecution of research aimed solely at contributing to knowledge have been denied access to official sources of information which could not possibly be classified as secret or even confidential. The usual reason given was that official information must always be treated as confidential. But if confidentiality was applied to its fullest extent then presumably the Registrar General commits a breach of confidence by publishing regular returns of the numbers of births, marriages, and deaths. However, there has in the last few years been a relaxation in the former rigid and hidebound attitude of officials towards the genuine requests of research workers for access to information and a more liberal interpretation of 'confidential'. The increased readiness of civil servants and local government officers to consider sympathetically requests for access to official sources of data from genuine research workers is distinctly encouraging, but there is, of course, the problem of the research worker who, having been given access to data, abuses the privilege he has received. There have been, unfortunately, in recent years abuses of this kind which must necessarily make the civil servants even more cautious, but it is hoped that research workers will not henceforth 'bite the hand that feeds them' because if the welfare state is to continue, and be improved, it is essential that a mutual relationship of trust between public servants and research workers is firmly established.

All too often the administrative mind fails to distinguish between essential, useful, and useless data. Harassed businessmen often complain of the obviously unnecessary forms they are required to complete before official approval can be obtained for some trivial transaction; farmers bemoan the endless hours they waste in making returns which to them seem pointless, and may suffer heavy financial penalties for having, for example, grown more potatoes than they were authorised to grow, even though, as happened at least once, there was a serious potato shortage; local government officers, hospital board officials, and the like continually grumble at the number of returns and reports they have to make which, according to them, seem to serve no useful purpose. And though many of these complaints may be unjustified yet typically British grumbling about officialdom, the fact remains that form-filling is looked upon as an essential concomitant of the welfare state. But, and this is what most of the emotional critics of the welfare state neglect to consider, in any administrative system—whether in industrial firms under a system of private enterprise or indeed in any other kind of organisation—communication through the written word is essential. One wonders, however, whether the use of forms and returns in central and local government departments has become an end in itself rather than the means to the end of policy-making. Administration seems all too often to be looked upon as a means of using the written word rather than making use of the written word to determine ends and means.

Many of the complaints about 'the paper war' waged in statutory organisations are nothing more than a whip used by critics unthinkingly to beat the concept of the welfare state. Those critics who are themselves businessmen might on occasion pause and consider whether copies in triplicate and reliance on 'files' are necessarily more widely used by administrators in statutory organisations than they are in industry and commerce, and, indeed, the professions. Equally, from one's personal experience of being passed on from one person to another in the course of a simple business transaction concerned with the repair of an ordinary household appliance, one often wonders whether the amount of unnecessary manpower in government circles is always greater than it is in industry and commerce. In short, it is usually unwise for people living in glasshouses to start throwing stones at their neighbours, and what is urgently needed in Britain now is for much greater attention to be paid to the fundamental principles and practices of administration in all types of organisations.

In those organisations commonly understood as being directly the result of the emergence of the welfare state, the collection and passing on of information from one person to another for what is euphemistically termed 'administrative purposes' has undoubtedly become a fetish. Hardly anything can be done without the use of paper and as the degree of control exercised by the central government over other statutory organisations has grown, so too has the quantity of paper consumed. It appears to have become axiomatic that control can only be exercised by the consumption of vast quantities of paper, and reliance of files and 'memos' becomes a disease which has now spread to all kinds of organisations. For example, in local authorities the quantity of paper consumed is all too often looked upon as a measure of the efficiency of the organisation, and ludicrous situations arise as in one county borough when the midwives protested vehemently against keeping such detailed records of the way they spent their time that they would, had they complied, have spent more time filling in forms than they would have on their essential task of attending to their patients. It would be interesting to know the quantity of paper consumed by statutory authorities in the past fifteen years, and even more interesting to know how much of it was really necessary.

It is extremely difficult to assess how much administrative waste there is and has been in the welfare state. The Public Accounts Committee of the House of Commons is a powerful instrument for exposing waste and inefficiency in the spending of money by government departments, and may even examine cases in which the administration appears to have been faulty or negligent,[8] but castigating a department will not necessarily reveal the person or persons who have failed in their duties. Under the doctrine of ministerial responsibility the blame for glaring errors on the part of administrators will be shouldered by the minister, and the real culprit may remain unscathed in his appointed grade until retiring age. This doctrine is a powerful weapon of protection for the administrator, but is it conducive to administrative efficiency, and in a welfare state, where errors may adversely affect the well-being of millions of citizens, ought there to be an added doctrine of public accountability for officials?

There is no need to adopt the practice of some countries in which officials are publicly upbraided and disgraced, often as scapegoats for corrupt and inefficient politicians, but there are limits to the extent to which any public servant should be given almost complete exemption from the consequences of his or her inefficiency. Human fallibility should always be recognised and forgivable, genuine mistakes may be pardonable, but sheer incompetence in doing one's job cannot easily be excused. And there is a dangerous tendency to extend the area of forgiveness and to enlarge the protective cloak of anonymity to limits which may well be contrary to the public interest. For example, doctors who enter into a contract of service with the state to provide medical services under the National Health Service Acts, and who are therefore in fact, if not in theory, paid servants of the state, may be punished by Executive Councils for seriously neglecting to fulfil their duties to their patients. The usual punishment is a fine, that is a part of the fees due to the negligent doctor will be withheld subject to confirmation by the Minister of Health, and the amount of the fine will be published in the press; but the name of the offender is never disclosed nor is he debarred from continuing in practice. The fact that a patient or many patients will have suffered through the doctor's negligence or incompetence is presumably taken into account in determining the amount of the fine, but in whose interest is it that he should not be publicly named? Obviously not that of actual or potential patients, who surely are entitled at least to be forewarned.

Doctors are not the only public servants who succeed in avoiding the consequences of their misdeeds. Recently it was reported in the press that a number of senior officials in a local authority had been claiming expenses to which they were not entitled, which is virtually the same as stealing public funds, but the names of the culprits were not published and all were apparently forgiven. The number of cases of these kinds is not very large. Nevertheless the fact that they occur and, even more important, that they obtain a special form of protection leads to the suspicion that in the welfare state more and more public servants are obtaining for themselves privileges and exemptions which could make them a race apart from the rest of the members of society whom they are presumed to serve.

The presumption that the duty of public servants is to serve the public interest may be quite unjustified because civil servants claim that their prime duty is to serve the minister, and local government officers aver that their duty is to serve the council, and there may well be a conflict between what is best in the long run for the public interest and what is best in the short run for the elected representative in power. Where then does the duty of the public servant lie? If to serve means no more than doing that which the elected representative asks to be done, and if this is all that we—the citizens—want our public servants to do, then we must be prepared to accept policies which may be designed primarily to secure political advantages and not the best interests of society as a whole. But surely to serve the government, central and local, must mean more than the public servant merely doing that which he or she is asked to do? It must include the provision of ideas about and views on existing, and the design of future, policies so that the politician may choose his course of action and accept political responsibility for it.

Critical assessment of present policies, and thinking ahead to the future, are functions which can only be carried out by persons not enmeshed in the minutiae of routine administration, and those in charge of research and development must have rank and status not lower than that of administrative heads. Objections will of course be raised against proposals of these kinds; the traditional administrator will argue that in government departments the making of policy and its implementation are indivisible functions; the politician will claim that it is for the party to make policy; and some taxpayers will recognise a dangerous tendency to increase the number of officials and give them greater powers than they already possess, which in any case are greater now than they ought to be.

Policy-making and its implementation are divisible, but they should be complementary functions; political parties will continue to propose policies but the party in office will have at its disposal objective assessments of the effectiveness or otherwise of its policies, and will still be politically responsible; and the tax-payer may well find that a drastic reorganisation of functions in government departments with a more rational distribution of responsibilities and powers will result in increased efficiency, better policies and practices, and even fewer power-conscious officials. Obviously we cannot, and ought not to, expect that all thinking about social policy should be left to civil servants, we need to use advisory committees and the like to produce social policies. We need, too, to encourage more public discussion so that more and more citizens can participate as has been suggested in the Skeffington Report.[9]

Whether we like it or not a strong, efficient, and imaginative public service is a *sine qua non* of any economically developed society. Totalitarian, democratic, laisser faire, and welfare states all need an efficient public service, whose members must inevitably be given powers. The degrees of power which public servants are allowed to exercise, and for whose benefit, are determined by the elected representatives of the people, and in a system of democratic government the possibilities of abuse of power can be controlled. We have developed governmental machinery with many admirable working parts, and we have succeeded in attracting into the public services men and women of undoubted ability and integrity, but all too often we have failed to recognise the need for adapting the machine to perform new functions, and that it must be operated by human beings who themselves require skills suited to the functions to be performed. The day of the amateur is over; running a public service and contributing to the making of policy have become highly specialised tasks requiring for their effective performance persons with outstanding intellectual and personal qualities. Many of our civil servants have these qualities, but because of the relentless character of the machine they operate, and the rigid hierarchical structure of the civil service, they have few opportunities to utilise their talents in the service of the nation. If we expect to go on attracting into the service persons of outstanding ability, then they must be offered the chance of interesting and challenging work, of a kind which is now more widely available in industry and commerce. The attractions of employment outside government service seem already to be creating problems of recruitment to the civil service and local government service is obviously not attracting the able grammar-school leaver as easily as it did thirty years ago. If the public service is going to get its quota of the ablest people in the country, as it must if it is to fulfil its responsibilities in a welfare state, then it must offer the prospects of a career which requires and allows intelligence to be used in an enlightened and satisfying manner. It is to be hoped that the reorganisation of the civil service on the lines recommended by the Fulton Report will lead to the right kind of recruitment, training and service because decisions in the welfare state, as in any other kind of state, depend on the right kind of people.

# Looking to the future 5

By the middle 1950s we, in Britain, had become accustomed to the idea that the welfare state had been firmly established, and that economically we were beginning to recover from the ravages of the Second World War and developing the so-called affluent society. Undoubtedly there was more affluence for more of our people than ever before in our history, but we were by no means economically strong and some doubts were already being raised as to the effectiveness and coverage of our welfare measures. The fact that more of us had better material living standards than in the past, that money wages were higher for more people, that the ownership of consumer goods previously restricted to the relatively wealthy was now more widely distributed so that even the working man (whoever he may be) had a car, a television set and so on, led us to believe that we had achieved the affluent society. For those, assumed to be a minority, who had not been fortunate in obtaining a fair share of the growing prosperity there was the safety net provided by the welfare state, so that the slogan 'you've never had it so good' really seemed to be true. But was it?

For some perceptive observers of economic and social affairs we had not achieved affluence or a welfare society by the early 1960s. Indeed, Michael Shanks argued that far from being economically affluent ours was in fact a stagnant society,[1] and for Professor R. M. Titmuss we had not achieved a welfare but an irresponsible society.[2] Michael Shanks suggested that our rate of economic growth had fallen behind that of every other developed country in the world, and that if we were 'to improve our economy to the point where we could achieve the same rates of growth as other Western countries ... and match the even faster growth rates of the Communist countries' we should have to reform drastically many of our long-cherished ideas about and attitudes towards economic activity and industrial relations. He believed that 'industrial democracy can go a long way to reducing inequalities of power and some way to reducing inequalities of status. It cannot, however, go very far towards securing greater equality of opportunity. But this inequality is, to my mind, the most damaging of all from the point of view of national welfare and efficiency'.[2]

Professor Titmuss was concerned about the 'changing concentrations of economic and financial power' in our economic and political systems and showed that 'as the power of the insurance interests (in combination with other financial and commercial interests) continues to grow they will, whether they consciously welcome it or no, increasingly become the arbiters of welfare and amenity for larger sections of the community'. He believed that the concept of the 'welfare state for the working classes' was largely a myth, and that there was little 'to suggest that much progress has been made, during the last nine years in which great fortunes have been accumulated, to concentrate help through the public services on those whose need is greatest . . . Those who have benefited most are those who have needed it least.' Inequality, far from being reduced, had been increased, and the concentrations of economic power he saw as 'accelerators of inequality' inequalities in the distribution of income and wealth, educational opportunity, vocational choice, pension expectations, and in the right to change one's job, to work in old age and in other spheres of individual and family need'.[3]

Whether conditions have changed drastically since 1960 is an open question.[4] Our rate of economic growth has certainly not greatly improved despite campaigns to increase productivity; a variety of fiscal measures to stimulate productive employment such as the Selective Employment Tax; control of prices and incomes through the National Board for Prices and Incomes; an elaborate national scheme for industrial training established by the Industrial Training Act 1964; full scale investigation into the relations between management and employees and the role of trade unions and employers' associations carried out by the Royal Commission on Trade Unions and Employers' Associations set up in 1965[5]; the establishment of Regional Economic Planning Boards and a host of other measures designed to accelerate our rate of economic activity and improve industrial relations. Some of these innovations may well need time to prove their worth, but what is abundantly clear is that the economy of the country must be strong if some of the basic aims of a welfare state are to be achieved. And perhaps one aim which aroused most discussion in the early 1960s was that of achieving equality of opportunity for all.

Those who see the welfare state as being designed primarily to reduce inequalities between individuals and groups are quite explicit about the kinds of inequality they wish to be reduced and, preferably abolished, but they are by no means as explicit about the degree of equality they wish to be achieved. Presumably reducing inequalities results in more equality and that in an imperfect world of imperfect human beings the only practicable goal to aim at is that of eliminating unnecessary and palpably unjustifiable differences in the opportunities afforded to individuals to live their lives. To suggest that all things could never be equal for all men at all times, or that all men would take equal advantage of equal opportunities and conditions at all times, is utopian. There are few protagonists of the welfare state who would make such claims, yet many critics of what they assume to be the welfare state as it exists in this country imply that the sole aim of the protagonists is to ensure absolute equality.

The two major political parties who have held office since 1945 are often assumed to be opposed to each other primarily because of fundamental differences in their attitudes towards the kinds and degrees of equality which the state ought to aim at achieving. The Conservatives accused the Labour Party of being interested only in equality. Thus Mr Iain Macleod in an article entitled 'The Political Divide', in a booklet published in 1958 by the Conservative Political Centre, *The Future of the Welfare State*, argued that 'there is another conflict peculiar to our times, which can also be reduced to a phrase or slogan: Opportunity versus Equality. These may well be the battle cries of the next election. If so, we should welcome it. Socialism, so Professor Lewis tells us, is about equality. It is a drab slogan, but then socialism is a sad creed. On our banners we will put "Opportunity", an equal opportunity for men to make themselves unequal.' Was the Labour Party concerned only with equality, and did the Conservative Party deliberately use the power of the state, during the years in which it was in office, to provide an equal opportunity for men to make themselves unequal? Never having been a member of either party, or for that matter of any party, and therefore never having taken part in discussions about policy at the seats of power, I am obviously not in a position to answer categorically these questions, but from reading pamphlets and books and the interminable speeches of politicians purporting to represent the aims and policies of both sides, and having observed systematically the kinds of policies preached and practised, I would not have thought that 'the political divide' was as clear-cut as Mr Macleod suggested.

An examination of some political publications reveals that there are occasions when it would be difficult to identify the political allegiance of the writers or to recognise the real political divide. For example, what is the fundamental difference between these two statements?

(*a*) 'It is no part of my argument to say that we should spend less on social provision. My argument, on the contrary, is that we should aspire to spend more, much more, and establish conditions in which our resources will expand to meet these aspirations. It does, however, seem to me that there is both a need and an opportunity now and in the years ahead for a major shift in the nature, direction, and emphasis of social spending ... towards modern services crying out for community effort or finance: namely the vigorous creation and maintenance by public authority of the finest environmental conditions for our people, and the generous application of public money to the subtler problems of personality, social adjustment, and education in its widest sense.'

(*b*) 'Looking to the future, there can be little doubt that what is needed is the direction of an increasing flow of savings into the British domestic areas of public squalor ... To raise the quality of environment for all our people should be at the very centre of social policy.'

The first of these two statements is from the preface to the Conservative Political Centre booklet *The Future of the Welfare State*, and was written by Mr Peter Goldman, Director of the Centre; the second is from the Fabian pamphlet *The Irresponsible Society* written by Professor R. M. Titmuss. Both are agreed on the need to raise the quality of the environment for all our people by social spending, presumably to make a better society for all, which is surely a fundamental aim of a welfare state; and there are many other aims which are held in common by apparently strongly opposed political writers. Where, however, there is a real political divide is in the means of achieving aims and in the interpretation of the ultimate effects on our society of using different means. There would seem to be at least two areas of fundamental difference in the means of achieving the well-being of individuals in society. The one concerns the role of the state, and the other (not of course unrelated) is concerned with the extent to which the availability and the provision of services conducive to individual well-being should be determined by the operation of market forces.

Much of what the state now does and ought to do is, apparently, not in dispute. A member of the Bow Group (founded in 1951 by ex-members of university Conservative associations) has argued that 'rigorous laisser faire is neither possible nor desirable' and it is one of the essential functions of the state to see that valid social interests are not neglected', but 'perhaps the most urgent and valuable task which Tories interested in the theories as well as the practice of politics can argue is this question of where we should draw the limits of state action. Not many can be said to have attempted it'.[6] Nor indeed, one suspects, have many Socialists or Liberals. In a democracy there are functional limits beyond which the state cannot go if it is to remain democratic, and in a welfare state there are presumably limits to which it must go if its welfare aims are to be achieved. All too often, however, discussions of the role of the state and the limits of its actions are bedevilled by the assumption that any extension of the functions of the state inevitably leads to a diminution in the freedom of the individual. Thus Mr Timothy Raison (*op. cit.*) argued that we had to make a choice 'between freedom or liberty for the individual on the one hand, and, on the other, paternalism by a government which claims that it knows best or feels that the rights of the individual can only be secured by a government prepared to intervene extensively'.

Is the choice quite so simple? Is it not possible that the liberty and freedom of the individual will in fact be increased rather than diminished by the actions of a government prepared to intervene extensively? Surely there are obvious examples in this country of where state intervention has substantially increased the individual liberty and freedom of the majority of citizens, and of where the rights of the individual could be secured only by extensive intervention on the part of the state. And there is, of course, always the possibility that too little intervention by the state will allow the many to be dominated by the few who may curtail the individual liberties of the many to an extent inconceivable in a democracy.[7]

The assumption that every extension of state intervention in economic and social affairs leads inevitably to restrictions on individual liberty and freedom is, surely, as yet unproven. We need far more systematic studies of the consequences of state action than have as yet been carried out before we can reach positive conclusions about their beneficence or harmfulness, and then we would be in a position to follow the excellent precept laid down by Mr Raison that 'one of the essential political principles of today ought to be that you should never act in ignorance if it is possible to act with knowledge'. And nowhere does this need to be applied more urgently than in that vast area of state activity, the provision of social services.

The differences in the attitudes of the main political parties towards the social services appear to be quite substantial. The views of some leading Conservative members of Parliament and of influential Conservative study groups have been explicitly stated in, for example, a pamphlet *The Social Services, Needs and Means* written by Iain Macleod and Enoch Powell; an article with the curious title of 'A Policy of Sewage' by Enoch Powell in *The Future of the Welfare State*; and an article in the Bow Group essays for the 1960s, by Geoffrey Howe on 'The Reform of the Social Services'. The predominant theme of these Conservative thinkers is that 'even in a prosperous society necessary claims on public expenditure can only be met if the social services, as we have come to know them, are drastically re-fashioned, so that their claims are diminished. Over the whole field of social policy our firm aim should therefore be a reduction of the role of the state,' but 'few Conservatives would doubt that the social services for the most part are here to stay. But we should hesitate to agree with Sir Keith Joseph who, while seeking "scope for sensible men to provide additional protection or amenity for their families and themselves *on top* of the state provision", plainly expects the state to go on making the basic provision for all of us for ever' (Geoffrey Howe, *op. cit.*).

The Labour Party and its supporters have been far less explicit in their published attitudes towards the social services, but Professor R. M. Titmuss has replied to the main Conservative views in chapter 2 of his *Essays on the Welfare State*,[8] and it would seem that the Labour Party sees the social services as an essential means of correcting social inequalities and that what is needed is more and not less social provision. The Liberal Party, in recent years, has also produced a series of policy statements indicating that they favour an admixture of private and social provision.

No political party has publicly declared that it is against the provision by the state of social services of any kind, though there are some individual writers like Colin Clark who would obviously like to 'denationalise' the statutory services[9] and the main area of dispute seems to centre around the extent to which individuals ought to provide themselves for their own welfare. The Labour Party clearly is in favour of communal provision, and social services should be provided as a right of citizenship and paid for by the community as a whole. The Conservatives on the other hand appear to believe that 'it is in keeping with the Conservative tradition to ask people to contribute to their own welfare and advancement', and therefore, for example, 'now that there is a demand for the grammar-school people may be expected to pay something for it'.[10] The essence of Conservative policy ought to be that 'a deliberate move must therefore be made towards the creation of a "self-help" state in which the individual is more and more encouraged to provide for himself and his family'.[11]

The Labour Party view is presumably based on the assumption that in an industrialised, capitalist, competitive economy the only possibility of ensuring a reasonable degree of equality of opportunity is through communal provision, and there is a fair amount of evidence which at the very least suggests that without communal provision of a variety of services our society would be very different today from what it is. Underlying the Conservative (and to some extent the Liberal) views there are a number of assumptions, for example, that services provided by the state are not paid for by individuals; that where an individual pays individually and directly for a service he necessarily has a different attitude towards and sense of responsibility for the service from what he would have if he paid indirectly for it through taxation; and that services paid for communally make us utterly dependent on the state and less responsible as individual citizens.

How valid are assumptions of these kinds? Obviously to assume that the state obtains its income other than from individual citizens or groups through taxation and other forms of statutory charges is untenable. The assumption that where an individual pays a share of the cost of communal services through taxation he has a very different attitude towards them from that which he would if he paid the market price directly out of his own pocket is still unproven, and raises a number of important and, as yet, unanswered questions. The theory is that if, for example, I am made to pay fees weekly, monthly, or every term for my son's education then I will have a different attitude towards and a greater sense of responsibility for education than I would have if the costs of education are met out of rates and taxes to which I contribute. Would I, and would most people? And does this theory imply that the whole costs of education must be met only by those who make use of education services? I cannot speak for everyone else in Britain (though it would be a relatively simple matter to find out the facts), but my own feelings and attitudes are quite positive: education is an essential service in a modern industrialised society; it should be a charge on the community as a whole; I have no objection whatsoever to paying taxes to meet the costs of education even though neither I nor my family may be using the services directly; the price of education ought not to be determined by the operation of market forces; and my attitude towards and sense of responsibility for education would most certainly not be improved by having to pay individual bills rather than making my contribution through taxation. And, furthermore, under a 'get-as-you-pay' scheme, what would the state do about parents who refused to pay for the education of their children?

The main debate in recent years seems to have been centred less on broad principles and more on whether the social services should be universal or selective. The universalists argue that, for example, education and the health services should be 'free for all' the selectivists on the other hand contend that those who can afford to pay part or all should do so. All sorts of ingenious (though not necessarily practicable) devices have been suggested such as vouchers and negative income tax.[12] The universalist versus selectivist argument is still far from resolved but the enormous variety of means (or needs) tests now in existence will obviously need to be drastically reduced if the selectivists' arguments prevail.

What of course we do not know is whether communal services make us less self-reliant and utterly dependent on the state. What proof does Godfrey Hodgson possess for his assertion (in the Bow Group essays, *op. cit.*) that 'one of the overall results of the individually attractive programmes of our political opponents has been to make the people of this country even more and more dependent on the universal provider (i.e. the state), and ever further from a sense of responsibility for its actions'? If this is true the electorate would be uninterested in what the government does and would presumably not bother to record its opinions at, for example, general elections. The fact is that, despite the ways in which governments since the war have created the impression of being more interested in retaining political power than in serving the needs of the nation, and the growing disillusionment of many citizens at the ineffectiveness of the House of Commons to provide a genuine forum for political debate, most of us do record our votes at general elections; and it may well be that if politicians treated us as reasonably sensible adults and not as morons more of us would show an even greater sense of responsibility for the actions of the state. Surely before making dogmatic assertions about the supposed effects on us as individuals of the actions of the state it would be preferable to find out what the citizens think and feel about, for example, the choice between communal and private provision.[13]

The belief that all 'public' spending is harmful whereas all 'private' spending is beneficial seems to be most widely held by those who assume that the amounts they pay in taxation are in inverse ratio to the benefits they receive from the state; those who believe that if Joe Bloggs, through no fault of his, receives more by way of 'benefits' from the state than he contributes in taxation then he is doomed to an attitude of dependence on the state and loses all sense of personal responsibility for everything; and those who believe that it is in the accumulation of private wealth as distinct from public wealth, and through the operation of market forces, that the best economic, political, and social interests of the nation are served. Thus Geoffrey Howe (in the Bow Group essays) argues that private wealth is 'an important equipoise to political power and a mainspring of economic expansion', a view obviously not held by Professor Titmuss who (in *The Irresponsible Society*) sees the growth in the economic power of 'the great insurance corporations' as constituting 'a major shift in economic power in our society. It is a power, a potential power, to affect many important aspects of our economic life and our social values in the 1960s. It is a power concentrated in relatively few hands, working at the apex of a handful of giant bureaucracies, technically supported by a group of professional experts, and accountable in practice to virtually no one'. For Titmuss the answers to the problems of achieving the best interests of the nation and reducing inequalities 'lie in many fields and forms of public ownership, public responsibility, and public accountability . . . To substitute the professional protest for the social protest and the arbitrary power of the City for the accountable power of the Commons is no answer'; a view shared by the Economic Editor of that sober and respectable Sunday newspaper the *Observer*, who, in an article on 'Tax Wealth, Not Gains' (8 April 1962), argued that 'excessive and growing concentration of money and power in very few hands is itself a threat to political and economic freedom'.

## LOOKING TO THE FUTURE

Serious study of the political and social history of this country over the past century provides little evidence to support the view that private wealth has been an important equipoise to political power. There are of course examples of individuals who have amassed great fortunes who seem to have had no interest in or effect on the distribution of political power, and have in fact used their wealth for the benefit of their fellow men. But in the complex society in which we live today can we, and do we want to, rely on the accumulation of private wealth as the means of ensuring the highest standards of individual well-being for all? Whether we want to or not we obviously in practice cannot, because we have reached a stage of economic and social development where even the richest individual or group could not finance most of the major projects which are accepted as essential for the maintenance of living standards. Indeed even projects which have no direct bearing on basic living standards are looked upon and accepted as being entitled to communal support. For example, when the Cunard Shipping Company had to face the problem of replacing the liner *Queen Mary* the ultimate decision depended on the extent to which the state was prepared to subsidise the capital cost of replacement, and there are a host of economic projects, far more vital to the nation than a prestige liner, which would never have been started, and certainly could not continue in being, without the support of the taxpayer.

While we persist in assuming that the accumulation of private wealth and private spending are in all respects beneficial and conducive to the public good, despite some evidence to the contrary, and that the accumulation of public wealth and public spending are in most respects harmful, despite the evidence of numerous indices of social and individual progress, so will all our discussions about the kind of society we would like ours to be and the methods of achieving it be obscured by charges and counter-charges based not on facts, but on untested assumptions and unsubstantiated beliefs. Much of the criticism against and much of the fervour for the imagined or actual welfare measures in operation in this country are based on partial knowledge, and often on sheer ignorance of what in fact they are achieving. To believe that they are only helping the feckless and shiftless and penalising the worthy, or bringing incalculable benefits to everyone, is to ignore the facts. And what we need to do, far more than we have done, is to search for facts so that we can devise policies based on knowledge of how best to serve the interests of society as a whole. But what are the best interests of society?

Much has been said and written in recent years of the deterioration in moral standards and in the sense of social responsibility of the British people. Those who make accusations of these kinds seem to direct their attacks against particular segments of society, especially those who are relatively defenceless, to have no sense of perspective or of the relationship of cause and effect, and themselves to acquiesce too readily in double standards of morality. One law for the rich and another for the poor may have been acceptable in the past, and could perhaps even have been justified, but it is not conducive to the development of 'one nation', which Mr Iain Macleod has assured us (in *The Future of the Welfare State*) it 'is the task of the Tory today to create'.

Our society is still riddled with differential privileges, powers, statuses and standards of conduct, which are incomprehensible to the enlightened visitor from abroad, and rarely do we pause to consider whether these differences are really necessary and in the best interests of the nation. Even more rarely are we prepared to examine objectively how other societies organise themselves and whether we could learn from them, despite our membership of international organisations regularly providing comparative data of a most useful kind, not least in relation to the provision of social services and methods of financing them.[14]

There are in our own country today people in high places and at the seats of power who believe that the burden of social service expenditure in Britain is heavier than it is in any other country, and yet numerous official reports from international governmental organisations, and even articles in reputable national newspapers, have shown conclusively that the financial burden is in fact far less here than it is in many other countries. Equally, it has been shown that social service benefits are often provided at a higher level in other countries than they are here, and that, for example, employers abroad bear a heavier burden of the share in financing social security than they do in this country.

Far more attention should be paid by politicians and administrators to the lessons which can be learned from abroad, and far more publicity needs to be given to the fact that Britain does not now lead, and never has led, the world in its attempt to establish a welfare state. Even ordinary observation would reveal that there are many features of our society which are not to be found at all or at most to a lesser degree abroad: our highly stratified class structure; our class consciousness and assumptions about the rights, duties, and privileges of the different social classes; our worship of pomp, ceremony, and tradition; our archaic ideas about employer-employee relations; our fear of economic planning and inability to clarify the role of the state; the high status we accord 'the professions' without really knowing what a profession is, and the low esteem in which we hold manual work; our outmoded system of local government and the false assumptions we make about local democracy; our respect for 'classical' education and relative neglect of scientific and technological education; and perhaps our greatest failing as compared with many other peoples is that we refuse to apply the principles of pragmatism.

It may well be that the avowed intentions of the Government since 1964 of 'modernising Britain' by encouraging scientific research and even to the extent of renaming the Ministry of Education the Department of Education and Science and establishing a Ministry of Technology have created a new climate of opinion more suitable to the world of the 1970s than that of the 1960s or 1950s. We cannot, as yet, be certain, but one must have doubts about the future when some of the Government's modern proposals have been rejected by powerful pressure groups as, for example, the resistance of the Trades Union Congress to legislation about 'wild cat strikes', and when it seems that much of the form filling of the past is still with us. Even in 1969 it was still necessary to obtain form P or S or X number so and so to obtain a relatively simple benefit, and the Child Poverty Action Group were surely right to point out the difficulties involved in obtaining the right form at the right time.[15] Is it really necessary in a welfare state to have so many forms and so many numbers for each form, and should communications between the policy makers, the administrators and the citizen be so complicated as they seem to be? I doubt whether they need be, and I am quite sure that the checking and re-checking, and checking again of forms within government departments is not only unnecessary but in fact quite expensive in terms of administrative costs. And, of course, the more form filling there is the more difficult it becomes even for the most intelligent citizen to find out what his rights are and how to obtain them. Rules, regulations, form filling and so on are a relic of the past and we clearly need now to decide whether they are all necessary.[16]

Despite some encouraging signs it seems that we are still at the stage where the natural inclination of British politicians, administrators, businessmen, and trade-union leaders is to despise facts and mistrust theories, with the result that the actual as distinct from the assumed situation in governmental and industrial fields is rarely closely examined, and theoretical concepts of possible courses of action are hardly considered. If scientists had been equally reluctant to search for, examine, and re-examine facts, and had refused to give serious consideration to 'theories' which at first glance seemed to have no possibility of practical application, then the material world of today would be very different from what it is. Scientific attitudes and methods are just as practicable and essential in trying to understand the problems of government, industry, and human relations as they are in discovering the secrets of nature, and if our educational methods had concentrated more on making us use our critical faculties and less on rote learning, then far fewer of us would be prepared to accept unthinkingly so many of our existing social, economic, and political institutions. And, of course, the growing power of the advertiser, and, more menacingly, the 'hidden persuader', would presumably not have been as effective in influencing the directions of our economic effort and the patterns of our social behaviour.

Advertising is no longer an essentially economic function; it has become a powerful political weapon. Every major party employs advertisers—euphemistically called public relations consultants—to exploit the party image, and to project a glorified image of the party leaders. National elections are fought not on the basis of the real differences between the programmes of the parties but on the most favourable image created by the advertisers, with the result that the voter has to make his choice from slogans and catch-phrases rather than from systematic policy statements of aims and methods of achievement. If the 'brand image' type of political discussion was confined to electioneering, then we might suffer it as we do other kinds of advertising. But there is a dangerous tendency for all political discussion and publications of party statements to be couched in advertising terms. Rational debates on the merits of rival party programmes are extremely rare, and even the House of Commons has virtually ceased to be a debating chamber. Issues vital to the nation as a whole are often discussed perfunctorily, and the most assiduous reader of *Hansard* would be unlikely to find from the reports of debates in recent years any consistent themes of the aims and policies of the parties for the present and future well-being of the nation. Indeed there is among many members of Parliament a growing awareness of the ineffectiveness of the House of Commons to control public policy, and there is a demand for radical reforms in parliamentary procedure. The promise to modernise Parliament made by the Labour Government has so far led only to morning sittings on occasional mornings. If there is no clear lead from the 'Mother of Parliaments' on the future policies of the nation, how are we, the citizens, to know which course to follow?

The Labour Party when in opposition published a report on 'signposts for the 'sixties', the Conservative Party was reported to be 'looking ahead to the 'seventies' and in 1969 the Liberal Party published a 24,000 word document entitled 'Liberals look ahead',[17] but none of these crystal-gazing exercises seem to have had much effect on the nature and structure of our society. But it is significant that the Liberal Party suggests that as far as the social services are concerned 'there should be no means test for the health services, education, and basic retirement pensions', though there should be 'strict selectivity in subsidies for housing and the encouragement of occupational pensions schemes'.[18] Does this, therefore, mean that we have now resolved the universalist versus selectivist argument?

One of the difficulties in deciding which way we go ahead is that we have not decided what we want our society to be. Do we want an 'acquisitive society' in which the material rewards go to the few who have the power to divert an undue share of the nation's resources for their own benefit, hence gaining more power and a status very different from the rest of us? Or would we prefer a society in which all had a reasonable share of the nation's resources, and differential rewards were based on responsibilities and contribution to the social good, and equality of opportunity a civic right? Apart from material rewards, on which even now we lay an undue emphasis, do we want the kind of society in which the few have rights and privileges denied to the many, or would we prefer to see privileges earned and accorded by society as a mark of distinction for outstanding contribution to the well-being of society? And so we could continue theorising about the kind of society we want ours to be, giving it a distinctive label such as 'welfare', 'acquisitive', 'protective', 'consumptive', 'competitive', 'egalitarian', 'elitist', 'permissive', and the like, but all too often using words without precise meanings or even defined limits. What, for example, is 'the social good', what are 'privileges', and what is 'power'? Each of us will have our own interpretation of words of these kinds, and concepts of 'liberty', 'individual freedom', and 'justice' are equally open to a variety of interpretations. We need far more precision in the use of terms commonly accepted as describing social objectives if we are to gain agreement about the aims and methods of achieving the best kind of society, and this requires far more knowledge about the structure and mechanisms of society, and about human relationships and aspirations than we have now, or are likely to have if we pay as little attention to social research in the future as we did in the past.

Framing social policy cannot always be delayed while exhaustive research is carried out to determine the facts on which to create policy; on the other hand policies should whenever possible and practicable be based on facts and not on assumptions and hunches. Politicians, administrators, and even hard-headed businessmen have a strange faith in the power of their own intuition, and they honestly believe that they know what other people think and desire even though the belief is based on very limited contact with very few other people. Only slowly have businessmen come to recognise the value of market research as a method of obtaining facts and opinions, and politicians and public administrators have only recently become aware of the potentialities of social research as a tool for the creation of social policy. The reluctance of politicians and civil servants to recognise that facts could be found, and the foolish position in which they found themselves as a result of not encouraging systematic research into the consequences of social action, was admirably summarized by Mark Abrams in an article 'Pattern of Welfare', published in the *Observer* on 16 April 1961. In that article Dr Abrams commented:

> When earlier this year the Commons prepared to debate the new health charges the Labour Party happily looked forward to great Parliamentary clashes which would restore the party's self-confidence and shatter that of the Conservatives. In fact, despite the noise, the attack would seem to have been completely ineffective. There were many reasons for this, but one of them was probably that moral indignation is no substitute for facts, and neither side was in a position to say quantitatively how many and which members of the public would be seriously affected by the new charges and how those hit might react. That the two parties should be in this state of ignorance is remarkable and deplorable. Currently the country is spending £3,000 million a year on the social services; a fair slice of this goes on providing each service with information officers and public relations units, but practically nothing is spent on finding out how consumers of these services use them and view them. Furtunately with a grant from the Nuffield Foundation, P.E.P. has now thrown some light on this neglected aspect of the workings of the welfare state.[19]

One hopes that the development of research units (or sections) within ministries and of the real interest in promoting social research through ministries and the Social Science Research Council will lead in future to the development of more firmly based policies. But it must be stated that some at least of the expensively financed social research projects in recent years seem to have little relevance to the real needs of society. However, it looks as though we have now entered a phase where policies will be decided more on the basis of knowledge and less on the hunches of politicians which should (we hope) lead to the development of more realistic and effective welfare state policies than in the past.

There is, too, the hope that the young people of the late 1960s and the early 1970s are less hidebound and more venturesome in their approach to and methods of social change. Despite obvious inequalities in educational opportunities, and the defects of our highly specialised and traditionalist education, young people today are more aware of the world around them than their fathers were, they are more eager to experiment and less conformist than previous generations, and of course there are far more of them continuing their full-time education beyond school-leaving age. It is unlikely that they will be content with a static society or that they will accept the dictum so commonly held by previous generations of parents—'what was good enough for my father is good enough for me and therefore good enough for my children'.

Those who castigate modern youths for their interest in material things, the way they spend their money, their lax morals, cupidity, and selfishness, seem to forget that these failings are not peculiar to the present generation, or to a single age group or social class. And if modern youth is in fact guilty of charges of these kinds could it not be that they are following the example set by their elders and supposedly betters? If working-class teenagers spend their money on exotic clothes, pop records, tape-recorders, and juke boxes, is this kind of expenditure so much less socially worthwhile than the vast sums spent on coming-out parties for debutantes? Are the misdemeanours of followers of professional soccer teams, who are constantly accused of damage to railway carriages when following their team to an away match, so much more harmful than the antics of the 'younger set' on the London underground after a coming-out ball? The proportion of teenagers from the 'working classes' who engage in anti-social conduct is probably no higher than that from the 'upper classes' whose conduct leaves much to be desired, and to stigmatise all the younger generation as irresponsible because of the behaviour of the few is to ignore the fact that the majority of young people today are, rightly, questioning the kind of society and the

## LOOKING TO THE FUTURE

world we live in, and have aspirations for the future very different from those of earlier generations.

The elders in the major political parties have already found that the younger members are not content simply to follow the lead given by their seniors, and when the younger no longer blindly accepts but questions and analyses the words, statements, policies, and practices of the older generation in power, then the nature, pattern, and rates of social change are bound to be different from what they were in the past. Our natural tendency to proceed by reform rather than by revolution will no doubt continue, but let us hope that they will be reforms based on knowledge, facts, ascertained needs and desires, and assessments of results. As the principles of scientific investigation become more widely known and applied to fields other than the physical and natural sciences, so will we recognise that many of the features of our economic, social, and political systems which we now accept as necessary, desirable, and inevitable are in fact unnecessary, undesirable, and certainly not inevitable.

There are still many people who question whether scientific methods can be applied to the problems of man in society, and there are others who make exaggerated claims on behalf of social science. Whatever views we may hold about the achievements of social science so far it can at least be said that social scientists are attempting to examine objectively the workings of society, and it is only through sustained and dispassionate examination of aims, purposes, functions, methods, and results that we can ever achieve a real understanding of the society in which we live, and enable decisions to be made as to the kind of society we hope to see developed in the future. In a democracy these decisions are made (or should be) by politicians within a system of representative government, and in a highly complex industrialised society the 'rulers' must have at their command facts on which to frame policy, and methods of measuring the results. Formidable tasks, but not impossible if the permanent officials, the paid servants of the state, are educated, recruited, and trained for the functions they must of necessity perform, and politicians recognise that they have a duty to society as a whole never to act in ignorance if they can act with knowledge.

A welfare state like any other cannot resolve all its problems. Crime, for example, persists and criminals are no less rare and as yet we have made little impact on the prevention of crime and the treatment of criminals. Perhaps one of the most urgent problems for welfare states in the future will be that of reducing the crime rate and dealing more imaginatively and constructively with criminals than has been the case in the past. But this is not the only social problem which remains to be resolved, there are many others which no state has yet solved satisfactorily and one can only hope that in welfare states at least solutions can be found more effectively and with less difficulty than in other kinds of states. The attempts which have been made since 1964 to deal with, for example, the problems of immigrants, with the needs of the elderly, with the recognition of economically depressed areas and of educational priority areas,[20] and so on, are indicative of a more imaginative approach to the needs of society than in the past. But, in the long term, we must decide what we want our society to be in order effectively to achieve our aims, and in a democracy it ought to be the citizens who decide the kind of society they want and the kind of government which will ensure the attainment of aims. The future of the welfare state depends therefore on us, as citizens, expressing our views as individuals, and in the numerous varieties of groups which we create to make known our collective views. What the future holds is difficult to foresee but it would seem as though the rate of social change is bound to accelerate so that even in 1980 our society and the role of the state will be very different from what it is in 1970, and certainly enormously different from that of 1930.

# References and further reading

In addition to the books and pamphlets referred to in the chapter references below, the following books provide interesting ideas about the concept of the welfare state in Britain and other countries:

Charles I. Schottland, ed., *The Welfare State*, Harper Torchbooks, 1967.
Gunnar Myrdal, *Beyond the Welfare State*, University Paperbacks, Methuen, 1960.
Piet Thoenes, *The Elite in the Welfare State*, Faber and Faber, 1966.
K. Slack, *Social Administration and the Citizen*, Michael Joseph, 1966.
D. S. Howard, *Values and Social Welfare: Ends and Means*, Random House 1968.

CHAPTER I

1. See Maurice Bruce, *The Coming of the Welfare State*, Batsford, first published 1961, third edition 1967, for comments on the controversies accompanying the social reforms of the nineteenth and twentieth centuries in Britain.
2. It has been suggested by H. and M. Wickwar in their book *The Social Services*, The Bodley Head, 1936, that the phrase 'social services' was first used by Sir Bernard Mallett to designate expenditure of this kind when he wrote in 1913 his *History of the British Budgets, 1887–1913*.
3. R. M. Titmuss, *Essays on the Welfare State*, Allen and Unwin, first published 1958, Chapter 2, in which there is an admirable discussion of the 'social divisions of welfare' and of the inconsistencies in the application of the term 'social services'.
4. *The Concise O.E.D.*, 5th edition, 1964. Curiously neither the *Dictionary of the Social Sciences*, ed. Julius Gould and William L. Kolb under the auspices of U.N.E.S.C.O., The Free Press of Glencoe, 1964, nor the *Dictionary of Sociology* provide a definition.
5. J. J. Clarke, *Social Administration*, 4th edition, Pitman, 1947.
6. Political and Economic Planning, *The British Social Services*, 1937.

7. M. Penelope Hall, *The Social Services of Modern England* (first published 1952), revised and edited by R. A. Forder, Routledge and Kegan Paul, 1969.
8. *Ibid.*, and see R. M. Titmuss, *op. cit.*
9. Adam Smith, *An Inquiry into the nature and causes of the Wealth of Nations*, first published in 1776.
10. For an interesting analysis of assumptions about what are social services see Titmuss, *op. cit.*
11. Iain Macleod and Enoch Powell, *The Social Services: Needs and Means*, Conservative Political Centre, 1951 and 1954. For a reply to these views see R. M. Titmuss, *Essays on the Welfare State.*
12. In the November 1962 issue of the Treasury's *Economic Trends* an attempt was made to measure who gains what from the welfare state, but it was far from convincing, and even the authors advised that caution was necessary in interpreting the results.
13. The Central Office of Information publishes a useful reference pamphlet, *Britain's Social Services*, published by H.M.S.O. and revised regularly.
14. See, for example, the reports of the Institute of Economic Affairs, such as *Choice in Welfare*, 1965.
15. 5 July 1948 was the much-publicised 'appointed day' for the implementation of the National Insurance Act 1946, the National Insurance (Industrial Injuries) Act 1946, the National Assistance Act 1948, the Children Act 1948, and the National Health Service Act 1946.
16. Quoted in R. M. Titmuss, *Problems of Social Policy*, the official history of the social services during the Second World War, published by H.M.S.O. and Longmans, 1950.
17. *Ibid.*
18. *Ibid.*
19. *Ibid.*
20. For an interesting and illuminating discussion of the impact of wars on social policy, see R. M. Titmuss, *Essays on the Welfare State*, chapter 4, *op. cit.*
21. W. H. Beveridge, *Full Employment in a Free Society*, Allen and Unwin, 1944.
22. In a White Paper, Cmnd. 6527, H.M.S.O., 1944.
23. It was, of course, Lord Beveridge who in the first decade of the twentieth century so plainly revealed that unemployment was an industrial problem.

24. In recent years political parties have often created the impression that they are concerned more with the retention or attainment of political power rather than with serving the best interests of society.
25. See especially T. H. Marshall, *Sociology at the Cross Roads and other essays*, Heinemann, 1963, and his *Social Policy*, Hutchinson University Library, 1965, for a good account of how individual rights have changed.
26. In the *European Journal of Sociology*, No. 2, 1961, Professor Asa Briggs in an article on 'The Welfare State in Historical Perspective' suggests that a welfare state is one in which organised power is deliberately used (through politics and administration) in an effort to modify the play of market forces in at least three directions, i.e. by guaranteeing income, by narrowing the extent of insecurity, and by ensuring that all citizens are offered the best standards of an agreed range of social services.

CHAPTER 2

1. On the meaning of social policy see T. H. Marshall, *Social Policy, op. cit.*, and J. L. M. Eyden, *Social Policy in Action*, Routledge and Kegan Paul, 1969; and for the making of social policy during the Second World War see R. M. Titmuss, *Problems of Social Policy, op. cit.*
2. Since the Ministry of Social Security Act 1966, the principles have perhaps been changed because now the citizen has the right to help from the Supplementary Benefits Commission.
3. See for example the recommendations of the Seebohm Committee—*Report of Committee on Local Authority and Allied Personal Services*, Cmnd, 3703, H.M.S.O., July 1968.
4. As it still is. More recently a measure of need based on average incomes has been suggested—see for example 'The Meaning of Poverty' by Peter Townsend in the *British Journal of Sociology*, Vol. XIII, No. 3, September 1962.
5. See B. S. Rowntree, *Poverty: a study of town life*, Thomas Nelson and Sons, 1901.
6. See the *Report on Social Insurance and Allied Services*, Cmnd. 6404, by Sir William Beveridge, H.M.S.O., 1942. For a very good study of the development of the system of social security since that Report see V. N. George, *Social Security, Beveridge and after*, Routledge and Kegan Paul, 1968.

7. See for example T. H. Marshall, *Sociology at the Crossroads and other essays* and his *Social Policy, op. cit.*
8. For a good account of the patterns and functions of different kinds of organisations see P. M. Blau, and W. R. Scott, *Formal Organisations, a comparative approach*, Routledge and Kegan Paul, 1963.
9. See again the Beveridge Report, and V. N. George, *Social Security, Beveridge and after, op. cit.*
10. For an account of how and why this system was created see *An Introduction to the Study of Social Administration* edited by D. C. Marsh, Routledge and Kegan Paul, 1965, chapter 5, 'Services for the Maintenance and Promotion of Health', by A. J. Willcocks; and A. J. Willcocks, *Twenty Years of the National Heath Service*, Routledge and Kegan Paul, 1967.
11. The latest proposals are those made by the Royal Commission on Local Government in England, 1966-69, under the Chairmanship of Lord Redcliffe-Maud which reported in 1969, H.M.S.O. Cmnd. 4040.
12. The Local Government Commission for England (and one for Wales) was established in 1958 under the Local Government Act of that year to examine the organisation of local government and make proposals for such changes as appeared to be necessary in the interests of effective and convenient local government. It has since been superseded by the Royal Commission on Local Government in England, 1966-69. See the Redcliffe-Maud Report, *op. cit.*
13. As indeed has been suggested by the Royal Commission on Local Government in England, 1966-69. See the Redcliffe-Maud Report, *op. cit.*
14. *National Health Service—the Administrative Structure of the Medical and Related Services in England and Wales*, H.M.S.O. 1968.

CHAPTER 3

1. For a good account of the Redundancy Payments Act, see V. N. George, *Social Security : Beveridge and after, op. cit.*
2. See V. N. George, *ibid.*
3. See again V. N. George, *ibid.*
4. Departments of Health and Social Security, *Social Insurance Proposals for Earnings-related short-term and invalidity benefits*, Cmnd. 4124, H.M.S.O., July 1969.

5. In 1964 the Schools Council was established which inter alia is concerned with ensuring comparability of examination standards of G.C.E. and C.S.E.; promoting curriculum development and research into educational problems. See its reports.
6. An attempt to set forth a policy for higher education was made by a Committee under the Chairmanship of Lord Taylor on behalf of the Labour Party. The report, published in 1963, is by no means clear about the nature of university education but seems to advocate an open-door policy. Even the long awaited Robbins Report does not make clear the real aims and purposes of university education, nor does it show the way in which universities are different, if at all, from other institutions of higher education. See the *Report of the Committee on Higher Education*, Cmnd. 2154, H.M.S.O., 1963.
7. See *The Youth Service in England and Wales*, Report of the Committee appointed by the Minister of Education, in November 1958, Cmnd. 929, H.M.S.O., February 1960. The chairman of the Committee was the Countess of Albemarle.
8. See the *Report of Committee on Local Authority and Allied Personal Services*, Cmnd. 3703, H.M.S.O., July 1968.
9. See for example, *An Introduction to the Study of Social Administration*, ed. D. C. Marsh, Chapter 5, 'Services for the promotion and maintenance of health' by Arthur J. Willcocks, *op. cit.*
10. See the Green Paper which was published to stimulate discussion about the future administrative structure of the medical and related services in England and Wales.
11. See, for example, a long list of books and reports on old people in *Some books on the Social Services*, published by the National Council of Social Service in 1969, and an article by Miss J. L. M. Eyden on 'Elderly people and the Welfare State' in *Social and Economic Administration*, Vol. 4, Number 1, 1970.

CHAPTER 4

1. See *The Civil Service—Report of the Committee 1966–68*, Cmnd. 3638, H.M.S.O., often referred to as the Fulton Report.
2. As was firmly recognised in France, for example, as early as 1945 when a remarkably thorough system was developed through the École Nationale d'Administration. For a comparison of British and French methods between 1945 and 1955 see *The Civil Service in Britain and*

*France*, ed. by W. A. Robson. For the proposed new forms of training in this country see the Fulton Report.
3. See the *Newsletter* published by the Social Science Research Council three times a year.
4. See Kathleen M. Bell, *Tribunals in the Social Services*, Routledge and Kegan Paul, 1969.
5. See *People and Planning*, Report of the Committee on Public Participation in Planning, H.M.S.O., 1969.
6. The proposals of the Fulton Committee, *ibid*, may remove these barriers.
7. *Report of the Departmental Committee on the Probation Service*, Cmnd. 1650, H.M.S.O. 1962.
8. In the Parliamentary Commissioner Act, 1967, we at last introduced the Scandinavian concept of the Ombudsman to give the citizen some rights of appeal against central government inefficiency.
9. See the report on *People and Planning, op. cit*.

CHAPTER 5

1. See Michael Shanks *The Stagnant Society*, Pelican, 1961, and R. M. Titmuss, *The Irresponsible Society*, Fabian Society, 1960.
2. Michael Shanks, *ibid*.
3. R. M. Titmuss, *ibid*.
4. Professor R. M. Titmuss in his *Commitment to Welfare*, George Allen and Unwin, 1968, is obviously still of much the same opinion as he was in 1960.
5. See the *Report of the Royal Commission on Trade Unions and Employers' Associations, 1965–8*, Cmnd. 3623, H.M.S.O.
6. Timothy Raison, 'Principles in Practice, Conservative Thought Today' in the booklet *Principles in Practice, a Series of Bow Group Essays for the 1960s*, Conservative Political Centre for the Bow Group, 1961.
7. See for example, R. M. Titmuss in *The Irresponsible Society, op. cit*.
8. And again in his *Commitment to Welfare, op. cit*.
9. Colin Clark, *Welfare and Taxation*, published by Catholic Social Guild, Oxford, 1954.
10. Godfrey Hodgson, *Education on Demand*, in the Bow Group Essays.
11. Hodgson, *ibid*.

## REFERENCES AND FURTHER READING

12. See for example the reports of the Institute of Economic Affairs on *Choice in Welfare*; Douglas Houghton *Paying for the Social Services*, Institute of Economic Affairs, Occasional Paper 16, 1968; D. S. Lees 'Poor Families and Fiscal Reform' in Lloyds Bank Review, October 1967, No. 86; and an article by Arthur Seldon on 'Which way to Welfare?' in *Lloyds Bank Review*, October 1966, No. 82.
13. One study made by P.E.P. on *Family Needs and the Social Services*, published by George Allen and Unwin in 1961 shows that a majority of the population favoured communal services. On the other hand some of the Institute of Economic Affairs reports suggest otherwise.
14. See for example the reports of the United National Department of Social Affairs, the International Labour Organisation, etc.
15. See a letter to *The Times* on 27 August 1969 from Professor Peter Townsend (Chairman) and Frank Field (Director) of the Child Poverty Action Group in which they also complain, rightly, about the enormous variety of means tests.
16. It is encouraging to find that in the White Paper on *Social Insurance proposals for earnings—related short-term and invalidity benefits*, Cmnd. 4124, published in July 1969, it is proposed that stamped cards will be abolished for all employees covered by P.A.Y.E. and the new contributions will be collected through the P.A.Y.E. system.
17. See *The Times*, 27 August 1969 for a summary of the Liberal Party Report.
18. According to *The Times* report of 27 August 1969.
19. P.E.P. report, *Family Needs and the Social Services*.
20. See the report of the Central Advisory Council for Education (England), published in 1967 and usually known as the Plowden Report, on *Children and their Primary Schools*, Vols. 1 and 2; and the report of the Central Advisory Council for Education (Wales) on *Primary Education in Wales* published in 1967, both by H.M.S.O.

# Index

Abrams, Mark, 103
advertising, 100–1
affluent society, 87
Albemarle Committee, 52–3

Beveridge Report, 1942, 6
Beveridge, William, 74
Booth, William, 2
Bow Group, 91–2, 95, 96

Central Office of Information, Social Survey Unit, 65
child guidance clinics, 52
civil liberties, 15, 16, 91–2
Civil Service,
   administration of, 63–5, 70–1
   duties and efficiency of, 61, 82–5
   staffing, 63–4, 74, 85–6
Clarke, J. J., 4
Cohen Committee, 19
crime prevention, 106
criminal and civil law, 15
Cunard Shipping Co., 97

defence, 15
'depressed areas', 24
doctors, 83

economic planning, 18–20, 87–9
   private wealth, 96–7
education, 4, 14–15, 48–52, 78–9
Education Act, 1944, 14

employment and unemployment, 13–15, 24, 27, 39
'equalisation grants', 34
equality, 87–90, 98

family allowances, 44
Family Allowances Act, 1945, 7
Fire Service, 15
'form filling', 80–2, 99–100
freedom of the individual, *see* civil liberties
Fulton Committee and Report, 61, 71, 74, 86

Goldman, Peter, 90–1
government, *see also* Civil Service,
   communications, 69–70
   human relations, 71–4, 105
   machinery of, 60–5, 67, 84
   official committees, 66–7
   relations between central and local, 75–6
government inspectors, *see* inspectors
Gowers, Sir Ernest, 71

Hall, M. Penelope, 5
Health Service, 3, 7
   administration of, 28–38
   Hospital Boards, 36
   lack of co-ordination, 54, 56
hospital services, *see* Health Service

# INDEX

housing, 3, 4, 15, 54
Howe, Geoffrey, 92, 96

income maintenance, 3, 4, 9, 15, 41, 43-4, 46
industrial injuries insurance, 44-5
industrial relations, 88-9
Industrial Training Act, 1964, 88
information,
  access to official, 63, 79-80
  statistics, 64-5
inspectors, 15, 76-8
insurance, 88

Keynes, J. M., 27-8

Lewis, Professor, 89
Local authorities and Health Service, 28-38

Macleod, Iain, 89, 92, 98
maternity benefit, 45
Ministries, *see* government, machinery of
Morison Committee, 78

National Assistance Act, 1948, 25
National Assistance Board, 28
National Assistance, rates, 25
National Health Service, *see* Health Service
National Insurance, 7, 43-8
  financing of, 41-3
National Insurance Act, 1911, 3, 24
nationalisation, 17
New Zealand, 47
Nuffield Foundation, 57

official information, *see* information
Official Secrets Act, 79
officialdom,
  contact with, 59
  power of, 68
Old Age Pensions Act, 1908, 3, *see also* pensions

'pay-as-you-earn', 43
Parliamentary procedure, 100-4
party politics, 18-19, 89-96
pensions, old age, 24, 44, 46
police service, 15
Poor Laws, 2, 23, 42
poverty, 2, 23-7
Powell, Enoch, 92
Prices and Incomes Act, 1966, 17
Prices and Incomes Board, 88
probation services, 77-8
protection of the individual, *see* civil liberties
Public Accounts Committee of the House of Commons, 82
Public inspectors, *see* inspectors
Public servants, *see* Civil Service

railways, 17
Raisin, Timothy, 91-2
Redundancy Payments Act, 1965, 40, 48
Regional Economic Planning Boards, 89
Rowntree, B. Seebohm, 2, 26
Royal Commission on Trades Unions and Employers Associations 1965, 89

schools for handicapped, 52
Seebohm Committee and Report, 38, 56

# INDEX

Selective Employment Tax, 88
Shanks, Michael, 87
sickness benefit, 44
Sheffington Report, 85
Smith, Herbert Llewellyn, 74
social reform and the State, 22–3, 89–93, 97–9
   determination of priorities, 27
   lessons from abroad, 99
   local and national administration 24, 28–38, 75–6
   statistical information for, 64–5
Social Science Research Council, 65
social services
   administration, 44–8, 53–6
   complexity of, 8–9
   definition of, 1, 4–7
   expenditure on and financing of, 4, 8–10, 62, 94–6, 98, 103
   future of, 101–6
   lack of statistics, 100
   outstanding problems, 57
   party policies, 85, 89–96

Social Work (Scotland) Act, 1968, 38
standards of living, 25–6
State control, *see* nationalisation
statistical information, *see* information
Supplementary Benefits 25, 41

taxation, 42–3
Titmuss, Professor R. M., 7, 11–13, 87–8, 91, 93, 96
Trade Boards Act, 1909, 3
Treasury, 60–2

unemployment, *see* employment
Unemployment Assistance Acts, 42

Water Act, 1945, 35

Youth Services, 52–3